Rosa and the Wolves

Rosa and the Wolves

✦

Biographical Investigation into the Case of Rosa Luxemburg

Ingeborg Kaiser/Translated by Patricia H. Stanley

iUniverse, Inc.

New York Bloomington Shanghai

Rosa and the Wolves
Biographical Investigation into the Case of Rosa Luxemburg

iUniverse books may be ordered through booksellers or by contacting:

iUniverse
1663 Liberty Drive
Bloomington, IN 47403
www.iuniverse.com
1-800-Authors (1-800-288-4677)

ISBN: 978-0-595-48962-6 (pbk)
ISBN: 978-0-595-49025-7 (cloth)
ISBN: 978-0-595-60910-9 (ebk)

Printed in the United States of America

Contents

Introduction

Rosa Luxemburg—specifically Róża (pronounced Ruscha) Luksenburg—the petite Jewess from Polish Ząmóść, emigrates from Poland at the age of 18, attains a Juris Doctor degree in Zurich, distinguishes herself in Berlin as a radical Social Democrat, as a merciless critic of the encroaching tendency to opportunism, conformity, nationalism, and militaristic thinking. Uncompromising even in prison, she cries out for resistance and revolution. On 15 January 1919 she is brutally murdered by reactionary officers. To Lenin she was an "eagle"; August Bebel called her a "poisoner." Today intellectuals are divided: "an icon of the leftists," *Spiegel* sneers; the Berlin magazine *taz* sees in her a "symbol of internal unity"; for the *Neue Züricher Zeitung* she remains "the Marxist theoretician ... who preached civil war," and for most people she is simply "Red Rosa."

In a conversation we had shortly before the publication of this book, Ingeborg Kaiser said, "Rosa Luxemburg is not a figure of yesterday. She is not finished. Then she was before her time, so now she has her place in the present. Her Utopia of internationalism is reality today."

She herself, the author notes, became aware of Rosa Luxemburg many years ago.

"My first approach to her was a slender book of *Letters From Prison (Briefe aus dem Gefängnis)* to Sonja Liebknecht. In these she does not complain. She narrates, consoles, and in extremely poetic language. That appealed to me, affected me very much. I didn't yet know that I would read the six volumes of her *Collected Letters (Gesammelte Briefe)* with the same fascination. Later I saw the Luxemburg film by Margarete von Trotta. I have never yet been able to forget the last image, the artificially lit Landwehr Canal at night. Then I began to buy political writings, and so on, almost without volition. My first Luxemburg text, *Don't Shoot (Nicht schiessen)* came out at the beginning of the 90s; I thought then about writing a stage play, composed a long prose poem ... so you see I have been circling the theme for a long time."

How does an author from a middle-class background come to create a comprehensive work about a person like Rosa Luxemburg, the radical Socialist maligned even today?

"I was very attracted from the beginning. After reading her letters and books I could empathize with her life, identify with it. It was a happy, strengthening experience. I admire her toughness, her will to persevere, her intellect, but I also liked her feminine sides.

"I'd like to add something regarding the term "middle-class." Looks have been deceptive up to the present. I come from modest family circumstances. My father was a minor official. My mother had very little means to see us through the month—the loss of fifty cents could become a drama for her. I liked to lose myself in daydreams. From our apartment I was able to see a large park with two splendid villas, gardeners and servants. A building contractor had inherited the property during a time of inflation, and I thought, when I grew up I was entitled to the same thing."

Has your image of Rosa Luxemburg changed in the course of your work?

"I began quite impartially. Her person soon grew larger, monumental, a giant-ess with whom I did not seem compatible. I expressed that, too, in my language, in hymn-like enumerations … In the course of my work this figure of the century came closer to me again. She had her weaknesses, too, made mistakes, was 'only' a human being."

Ingeborg Kaiser approaches the historical figure of Rosa Luxemburg on three different levels that are clearly separated from each other in the book and that are always clearly recognizable to the reader. On the first level certain situations in the life of Rosa Luxemburg, available in letters, documents, and information in the secondary literature, are objectively reconstructed. In these sections the author remains, however, visible as a subjective observer.

Level Two takes note of the experience of numerous trips that Ingeborg Kaiser undertook on the trail of Rosa Luxemburg. Her chief goals are: Berlin, where the revolutionary exerted her greatest effectiveness and where she died; Zamóśe, the town of her early childhood; Warsaw, city of her youth, her first revolutionary experiences, her first prisons; Wronke and Breslau, where the prisoner in protec-tive custody was held during World War I; and Auschwitz, where Luxemburg's friend, Luise Kautsky, and her longtime co-worker Mathilde Jacob were mur-dered. Here, most of all, it is obvious to what bestiality that German inhumanity finally led. Luxemburg fought it all her life and she herself fell to it. In all these passages personal experience is mixed with intensive investigation of Rosa Lux-emburg's life circumstances.

On the third level, finally, something like an interior dialog develops between the narrator and her figure, who at these times is familiarly addressed as Róża

(Ruscha). These are mostly short moments of existential solidarity in contrast to the historical documents. A narrative sideline belongs to this level also, it blazes up sporadically but is to be read as an invisible underground of the text. Images from the time of World War II, the narrator's childhood impressions—they also verify how legitimate Luxemburg's warnings of the National Socialist inhumanity were. From this second narrative thread a third branches off, the history of a certain Rehn, who enters as a volunteer in World War I and in World War II serves as a postal official in occupied Poland, where he witnesses National Socialist crimes. This figure is, on the one hand, a compositional counterpoint to those passages which narrate the prison life of Rosa Luxemburg. On the other hand they stand for all people who were not reached by her message.

The aforesaid conversation with ingeborg Kaiser touched also on formal questions:

Is *Róża und die Wölfe* actually a novel?

"In any case it is not a biography. The text is probably difficult to categorize."

If we remain provisionally with the concept of novel, is it a novel about Rosa Luxemburg or a novel about Ingeborg Kaiser?

"The theme is Rosa Luxemburg, but the author is clearly participating by means of the process of personal rapprochement represented in the book and by means of what she relates to Róża."

How did you develop this very special form with its different levels and the broken chronology?

"It was necessary to separate the historical figure of Rosa L, who is austerely portrayed in documents, from Róża, with whom I can also speak privately. The structure of the book was given in the 'Berlin' chapter. In Berlin Rosa L. worked, she was a prisoner there, she was murdered there. The titles of the following chapters—always city names—are a constant cue to the time when Rosa L lived there. What is narrated relates to that time. And also, it is a strict organizing principle, though not chronological."

Rosa and the Wolves is a very artistically composed book. With uncanny sensitivity the author changes the course of the report, shifts times and perspectives, incorporates quotations, alternates from one level to another, so that an oscillating tension arises between the record and the object of the narrative. This type of participation and withndrawal from participation always characterizes the literary creations of Ingeborg Kaiser. Anyone who knows her earlier novels, from *Die Puppenfrau* (translated as *The Puppet Woman*) and *Regenbogenwahn* (translated as

Rainbow Madness) and *Mord der Angst* (translated as *The Murder of Anxiety*) up to *Den Fluß überfliegen* (translated as *Leaving the River*), her tightly knit stories, her discreet poems, will be astonished how much this "imported woman"—the way she describes herself in the short story "Eingeschleust" (translated as "Smuggled In")—does not hold back from revealing her own personality in *Rosa*. Although the "Investigation" is certainly not a "novel about Ingeborg Kaiser," as a story of rapprochement, of a fantasy friendship, if one will, it has two main figures, Rosa Luxemburg and the narrator.

Riehen/Basel, May 2002
Valentin Herzog

Berlin

1. A windy day in January. Identical blocks of apartments in the gloom as ifbuttonedup, faceless, a faceless city sector where the Greek restaurant stood out bright and exotic. I went in, happy to escape the frosty wind and to be able to await the evening's talk of Rosa in southern ambience. Outside the window a thickly branched winter tree that did little to obscure the view of the Prussian Main Cadet Academy on the other side of the street. Feathery clouds swift over its roofs. A city behind shingled walls with a broad iron gate and a porter's box, fronted by the heavily trafficked encircling street. Spotlights like cats' eyes flared up, disappeared.

In 1878 the first thousand cadets moved into the red brick buildings behind walls, a place of cultivation under alternating flags and uniforms. During the Weimar Republic higher education students succeeded the cadets, later Hitler's SS guards. In the summer of 1934 a place of activists. After the murder of SA-leader Röhm fatal shots were fired here on men who had become inconvenient. One world war more and the Star-Spangled Banner of the American rescuers waved above "Andrew Barracks."

Today its walls house the national archive of the unpublished papers, including those in the GDR, of Rosa Luxemburg, the Jewish Pole and revolutionary who was murdered but not silenced. The writings and letters of this articulate politician are still fascinating. Her life a too quickly run film with rapid scene changes, a history of great feelings, of war and resistance, of love, despair, of faith in oneself. This woman without a home, indeed without a country, became a sheltering receptacle for ideas by which one may remain a human being with all its contradictions.

The friendly Greek cleared away my half-full plate, a dish too fatty at the wrong time. Rosa L's nervous stomach would also have rebelled, I suspect. A little feverish before the exhibit of the Rosa Luxemburg documents and meeting Rosa Luxemburg experts. In a dialog with her writing for a long time, I had become intimate with her as if with someone with whom I felt comfortable, curious about everything in her life, her history, the traces of which I followed. As if Rosa L.'s life were intermingled with mine, if history were repeatable. The Polish Róża or

1

Ruscha interested me along with the historical figure of Rosa L. that was painted in numerous very knowledgeable biographies. She permitted me to play the game of possibilities, speaking to her familiarly and as if she were in the present time.

The gate across the street stood open, the first visitors were already waiting at the porter's box, and my Greek wished me a pleasant evening, which belonged to Rosa L. To her unpublished papers, which were to be viewed on the eve of a scientific conference of the International Rosa Luxemburg Society in the national archive.

The lighted windows of what was earlier the garrison church reminded me of a gilded Christmas card with worshipers making a pilgrimage to High Mass through the crystal sheen of a snowy night, but these were researchers and friends of Rosa L who were here for a special yearly meeting. Soon they would bend over glass cases, turn pages in the album of a life, stop before an image and discuss it as carefully as if their future were dependent on it.

The military lockers in the visitors' cloakroom had outlasted decades and evoked images of uniformed men lined up to receive a command: baby-faced cadets convinced of the goals of their Emperor; later a commander with a propensity for brutality, with SS-script and a skull on his cap, who will march stiff-legged into the nameless "Front" of the Black Corps. And the brown shirts of the Röhm affair, who will be drenched in blood, and a good decade later a dark-skinned GI with chewing gum, Lucky Strikes, and chocolate will buy an hour of love.

The bookcases and reading tables in the church nave seem to be placed there incidentally. They can just as incidentally disappear overnight, as the men in the century of two world wars disappeared, without a sound, without justice, without a face, one above the other in the varying slaughters on the stage of time.

Your life, Róża, like a darkened icon, varnished many times over. The colors unchanged in the light, mirrored in the faces of visitors. But this was no nostalgic hour of private prayer in the church nave of yesteryear. The audience too diverse, their only unanimity their admiration for a great woman and a life that became history.

The Japanese professor at the lectern held a new publication in his hand, your sternly beautiful face again on its cover, to many well known, a public face, Róża, as public as individual sentences from the volumes of your words, which when repeated sound like classical music in a supermarket. And your life's work? Still just a wrinkled body in a corset of quotations?

Prussian austerity in the nave, above the heads of the listeners two large, dimmed chandeliers, the meager glow of electric candles repeated in the white-washed walls. In the Romanesque arc-ed windows the blackness of night, locked out by the light geometric bars of the windows. A globe on a bookcase in the distance, Europe must swim on its northern half, splintered by the numerous countries. The boundaries of the old world, unstable as shifting sand dunes exposed to the wind of time.

Socialism unbridled, its Utopia of equality dissolved by increasing inequality. Rosa Luxemburg's estate was now an archive of the federal government but with GDR archivists. Blonde rosy-cheeked Brunnhildes in severe costume presented their work, in between the lightning flashes of a photographer's camera. *The world is so beautiful despite all its horror*, Rosa L., wrote from protective custody in the wintry fortress Wronke. The sentence now serves as a title on the new coffee-table book. On its cover the portrait of Rosa as a promising high school student standing before a Spring-bright backdrop.

The small group of Rosa L. friends, exposed to the icy needles of wind, waited for the last bus. One woman headed purposefully for the Greek's. She peered through the bright window and turned away annoyed as if she had seen too much pampering in the shadow of the red brick Prussian walls. The bus a comfortable cave. A petite passenger, bundled in a floor-length coat and seated in the farthest seat fixed her old knowing glance on the newcomers. Mostly robust women exuding self-assurance for whom Rosa L. was a champion. As they did every year on the anniversary of her death they would thoughtfully walk her path to death and in the evening throw flowers in the Landwehrkanal. They invited me to accompany them, curious what chance affair had brought the stranger to Berlin. Perhaps it was a love situation that had made her a traveler, an idea that she indulged but did not want to explain.

Arrived yesterday. The moon accompanied my night journey, battered but true, the sound of wheels turning and a rocking sensation in the sleeping compartment, sometimes the sight of deserted railroad stations filled the window in the harsh artificial light, swiftly released from the land of night, extinguished. Speed a light rustling of wind-song that pierced the distance as I listened, was a thing that was transported on rails over borders, time and space conquered without my help. More comfort, more speed than the traveler Rosa L. had, but the danger greater, the tiny sleeping compartment with deadbolt and a chain for security. Towards morning the wake-up knock, breakfast, travel papers, everything recorded, the arrival at Bahnhof Zoo punctual. The travelers shoved step by step through the narrow auto corridor. With my bulky suitcase I was a hindrance, angered those being pushed behind me. The porter waiting at the exit seemed to me like a messenger sent by Rosa, only without wings.

A frosty morning. The stream of arrivals pushed their way down the steps to the exit, sucked into the traffic of a metropolis. I waited with the porter for the glass-enclosed giant of an elevator that swayed with a young woman in a long black skirt, short mauve jacket and darker leather gloves; her face behind a veil, she stood motionless in the middle of the elevator. When the porter with his heavily laden cart stopped directly on top of her, she rolled over. My warning scream would have been to no avail, for there was nothing, the young woman disappeared.

Cardinal red the sky above the tall roofs as I was driven over the city's highway and actually did not want to arrive anywhere. But the key fit in the lock of Number Thirteen. Traversed a well-cared-for "Jugendstil" house, a spacious courtyard in back, a house back there before one reaches the single story little house among the trees that stands between long drawn-out lines of rental houses. And stories could be told of the coachman who lived there with one or two horses under his roof when the twentieth century began and Rosa L. lived in the city of two and a half million population.

2. She was exactly twenty-seven years old when she moved to Berlin in May of 1898 and knew what she wanted. Dr. Rosa L. had successfully concluded her years of study in Zurich and Paris with a work on the industrial development of Poland. And was on her way to join the party of August Bebel and Wilhelm Liebknecht, to become active in the Socialist movement. She would soon hear that she was a young upstart at a Party rally revisionist debate by merciless old members. She would give a glowing account of herself as a highly intellectual rhetorician. She was no longer a greenhorn, although she had no rank within the Party, as she noted ironically.

The eighteen-year-old Rosa L., as a member of a Polish underground movement, had to flee illegally over the German-Polish border. She had come to Zurich, her doctoral advisor, Julius Wolf, sensibly remarked, as a full-fledged Marxist, here during her student years she had resumed her Polish work with her lover Leo Jogiches and the other emigrants. As editor of the newly founded newspaper "Sprawa Robotnicza" ("The Workers' Business") an organ of the SPD in Poland, she soon also published in influential German Party papers. Meetings with leading Socialists in Paris and her first appearance at the Socialist Congress in London brought her a great deal of attention.

Berlin a city of farewells for Rosa L., this time of her own free will, as it seemed, however it was farewell from the comfortable island of Switzerland, where she had felt good, from friends and lively experiences with Leo, her beloved "Dziodzio," who remained in Zurich to complete his studies. Wouldn't it be happier, she wrote from Berlin, if instead of leading such an adventurous life, she could enjoy her youth quietly and heartily somewhere in Switzerland with Leo. But she suspected that Leo, Polish revolutionary and clever conspirator, lacked the talent for happiness away from the action, that her love was an illusion, although she had the damned desire to be happy and would also be ready to haggle for her little portion of happiness. But life could grab and not let go.

Rosa L. was ready, although even the first few hours in strangely cold Berlin exhausted her completely. She compared the city to a military barracks and had a premonition of the stick with which she was once whipped behind the arrogance of the kind Prussians. Actually, for life here Rosa L. needed a reserve of health and strength far different from what she had brought with her. She rode the streetcar to search for a place to live, in a few days saw seventy-five rooms and rented one in the most aristocratic part of the city, near the zoo, and by three Marks too expensive, but it did not smell of military officers.

I am certain that you yourself would have chosen what I chose, and that soothes me.... But write immediately so that I can know you will not scold me too much because of the three Marks.

With bookkeeping exactitude she justified her choice to Leo and compared the necessity for that outlay of money with other offerings. The room was elegantly furnished, with an upright piano, desk, rocking chair, a mirror over the entire length of the wall and colossal sleep sofa, a sink behind a colorfully coordinated curtain. On top of all that, the little green balcony, luxurious greenery all around it, and clean air.

Self-confidently she sought out the SPD party leadership, became a member of the Party and offered her services for the election campaign in progress. Instead of Westphalia, as she imagined, she was ordered to Upper Silesia and successfully informed the Polish speaking population of election issues. Along with that she accelerated the issuance of a local identity card at the police headquarters on Alexanderplatz with the aid of a three-Mark tip.

Rosa L, the Polish Jewess from Warsaw with the little limp had not become a Prussian citizen without problems. She needed the right papers in order to be able to do political work. Her fictitious marriage to Gustav Lübeck of Berlin had taken place a few weeks earlier, in April 1898, in a civil ceremony in Basel.

The photograph in the Zurich studio on that day shows an energetic little person with dark hair, her arm linked with that of her fictitious husband, who was wearing a high hat that towered over her. The machinist's large hand entirely covers the little hand of his wife, without possessing it. She is wearing a high-necked dark wool costume. The jacket's many buttons emphasizes her tightly belted waist, the bell-shaped skirt allows just the tip of her shoe to be seen, and an elegantly draped hat emphasizes the closed face with its dark eyes.

One hundred years later colorful balloons on the "Day of the Open Door" enticed the public into Basel's Civil Status Office near the cathedral towers. Under glass the marriage papers in Rosa Luxemburg's handwriting that identify her as a *former writer*. An additional hand-written letter from Rosa L arrived a few days after the marriage ceremony in the Civil Status Office in which she applied very politely to correct the profession of Gustav Lübeck, who no longer worked as a machinist, to businessman. It was rejected.

What was the reason for this attempt? There is no conclusive answer, just possibilities. Certainly no conceit was involved, although at this time it was hardly creditable that a full-fledged female doctor would marry a worker. Perhaps it was Leo, who, looking ahead, considering her planned entrance into Berlin, wanted to improve her biography.

The singing of the approaching fast train and the weighty horns of the ambulance brought me back to the present, to January in Berlin. The flickering light a promise in pink and blue sounds. Swiftly the corridor of sky darkened above the long façade of the rental house, the diagonal brick wall disappeared, the raven's nest held securely by limb fingers in the windblown treetops. The glassy eyes of brightly lit apartments showed shadows puttering about in tunnel-like kitchens, not far off the glimmering blue of the TV. A door to the back yard opened, the white Pomeranian pranced a little in the artificial light, followed the inaudible call of its owner into the house. An Oriental carpet runner was taken down the steps from the terrace of the first floor into the back yard area. The small shops in this quarter, many of them run by women—one exception the anonymous, neon bright laundromat—crowded together. The flower kiosk, the sewing studio, the stationery store, hair salon or the wine shop, where the comfortable connoisseur with a bottle in her hand also gave out friendly advice. Across the street a show window on which I pressed my nose flat in order to spot more of the tunnel of shops. Behind the dark corpus of merchandise, lit by two chandeliers, a rich selection of materials for every occasion, rolled-up bales stowed in shelving that reached to the ceiling.

And I conjured up Rosa L. among the bales of material as she carefully selected yellow or cream colored silk for a dress and sought out a seamstress. The shoulder section of her blue dress was completely discolored to yellow by sweat, she wrote to Leo. She would have the dress altered with a silk substitute, as was fashionable now, and the dress would be chic. She would take it with her to the Party meeting in Hanover and wear it on the social evening, and freshen up the blue hat from Zurich with a white ribbon, because the old one was dirty. For the yellow silk she would have to count on paying 23 Marks to the seamstress for the work, the trimming, and accessories.

Since you are placing money at my disposal, I have also ordered a new corset (the old one split along its entire length and is beyond repair).

She knew that a good-looking wardrobe would support the initial impression she made. The black with a corsage for the evening with old Bebel and also perfect for her appearance at assemblies or before the court, complemented with gloves and hats. Elegant hats, pretty linens, shoes, the silken blouses white, striped, or black, mostly dark skirts, her Paris coat of blue silk.

The announcement of her purchases and money outlays are mixed in with reports to Leo about her daily political work, proof of the intimacy between partners in life as well as politics. The epistolary tone to *dear Dziodzius* at the beginning of the century sounded bold, pert, tender, impetuous, or insistent, and in any case unconventional. Leo's family in Wilna owned a prosperous mill and properties. He lived on funds inherited from his grandfather and could effortlessly supplement her meager income, despite her scruples. The conscientious listing of her outlay reminded me of a housekeeping book in my childhood, where nothing was ever spent that could not be justified. Remembered, too, the child Róża in Warsaw, who innocently lit a lamp with the last piece of paper money the family had but was consoled by her father, who dismissed the bitter loss with a joke.

3. I had nodded off to sleep when tobacco smoke woke me. My nocturnal visitor sat with her legs drawn up on the library sofa. On the floor a bottle and two glasses. Tentatively the unknown woman looked at me and left me time to regard her as well as she huddled there so comfortably. The harlequin scenes on the three wooden tablets that covered the wall behind her made a fitting backdrop for the woman's acid green outfit, her green lacquered page-boy hair, the olive-colored painted mouth, her green eyebrows. As if she had—ageless—climbed down from one of the images in order to be noticed finally. She stubbed out the cigarillo, fingered with long green lacquered nails the next one and lit it. Silently I

turned to the desk and wrote a name on the paper, always the same, one after the other: Róża, Ruscha, Rosa L, and hoped that the green woman would disappear as noiselessly as she had come.

But she reached for the uncorked wine bottle, poured a drink, took a few sips.

"Why dig up what is dead," she said, "as dead as Rosa? I can't hear anything more about it, time swept away the firebrand and her Spartakists long ago. And no resurrection, just simply gone. No one is curious about what was then. Who knows any more about her, the blue flower of the Reds, and her splendid end as fish food in the canal. Such a plant doesn't belong in the herbarium, lovely behind glass. It does nothing for me, or just as little as lovely sentences that are only lovely but don't say anything. I am a proletarian, I need something else, today is more important to me than turning back the pages of time. Anyone coming from over there won't let himself be hoodwinked with slogans any more. The "Red Rosa" was their figurehead, for me she is a dead woman who has nothing to do with me, and I don't see what you would have to do with Rosa.

The torrent of words awakened me. While she was still talking I had an answer, many answers, all of which I discarded. As if I wanted too quickly to babble something that concerned only me without trying to explain an image that I have regarded for a long time, without being able to lay a foundation for what attracted me.

"Your Rosa," I could have said to my surprising visitor, "is a clone decked out in the ideologies of the former GDR fathers. Whoever lived over there, believer or non-believer, was nothing but fodder for propaganda and had to swallow too many -isms. Your one-eyed glance at Rosa L. can grasp nothing of her multifaceted personality. But what's to be done. Everyone is molded by some kind of -ism created by the opposing view; who can absolve himself?

"Rosa L is not decayed. Her life is history, a limb of the century tree, with various and sundry branches, to remove it would cripple the tree, falsify history. What is time, after all, only constant flux, and what does being dead signify to someone who means to live? My today needs the knowledge of yesterday, and the memory and the voices of the dead enliven the present. The voice of Rosa L. is familiar to me, has been since I have learned about her, her writings sharpen my private view of our time. Nothing is apolitical," I could have said, "the individual is part of a world, always concerned with its events, it doesn't matter where they happen.

"For a long time two photos of barred windows hung on the wall in my room. They corresponded at the time to my feelings about life, and they reminded me of Rosa L., the prisoner under protective custody. Her cell, from the point of view of the one enclosed in it, stripes of light brighten only sparingly the shadowy space. In the other photo the barred window is the central image, the strong light from the south seems to melt away its iron rods. Two pictures by two photographers, a woman and a man who do not know each other, completed a pictorial history that I frequently read. And remembered the four-year-old child who ran away every day and was finally locked up by her mother in the cellar of a shed belonging to the office and apartment building. In a neighboring shed the lament of an arsonist, but the child threw herself against the bars of the cage and soon forced her mother to let her out.

"And also the image on the movie screen perversely lovely, the last frame in the Margarethe von Trotta film, the view in the darkness of night of the canal seen from the bridge railing. The silent stream, shimmering in artificial light, a flowing grave over which the water's skin closed like a movie curtain. An image that enticed me as if it were possible to part the water, as if Rosa L. had left behind for the fish and algae a last message that was still to be lifted out."

I must have spoken aloud and woke as a result to a dawn light from which the contours of the room and its things slowly advanced, no trace of my nocturnal visitor except for my memory and the faint tobacco smoke, which the last renter could just as well have left behind. The light beyond the window a cold gray, roofs wet with rain, the first lights in the row of houses.

4. A polar wind swept through the streets of Berlin-Friedenau. But the group with its briskly striding city experts headed for several locations where Rosa Luxemburg had lived and worked; they appeared immune to the biting cold. The middle-class boarding house with balconies in Wielandstrasse was Rosa L.'s fourth address. Coming into view a well-cared-for corner house where the influential Karl Kautsky and his wife Luise, their three sons and grandmother Minna had occupied the top floor. The background of houses on both sides with rows of trees seemed created by a stage designer who knew the play and its performers, who would unavoidably meet each other here.

The young, strong-willed Dr. Rosa L. and the committed, mostly masculine politicians with their chairman August Bebel at the hospitable table in the Kautsky home. A friendly gathering, but not without quarrels.

I know them (...) already like my five fingers. (...) And I don't value all this combustibility and the invitations overly much, and they always asked me three times before I approached them.

In a few months she had made a name for herself with her writing in the big Social Democratic presses like *Vorwärts* or *Leipziger Volkszeitung*, was quoted and reprinted. At her public appearances the enthusiastic speaker was admired and also feared. A comet-like ascent that made her self-confident and proved that she had persuasive powers but at the same time split open her personhood into that of an ambitious politician and that of a lover, who reported to the distant Leo her discontent with the wretched band of Party members, the closed circles, the gossip mongers, and the burdensome invasions of her privacy by her near neighbors, the Kautskys. She dreamed of a personal life with her beloved, of their own little apartment with their own furniture, their own library.

Calm and regulated work, strolls together, now and then the opera, a small, a very small circle of acquaintances whom one invites to dinner from time to time, each year in summer a month-long trip to the country, but entirely without work! (And perhaps also a little, very little Bobo? Will it never be permitted? ... Oh, Dziodzu, will I never have a Bobo?!)

As a matter of fact it was definite; for the revolutionary Leo private happiness was of secondary interest. And Rosa L. would again and again renounce *that which one personally would like,* the politician holding back the lover, although at twenty-eight now she compared herself to a cat that would like to be stroked and to stroke others. She enjoyed being spoiled by her Berlin friends on her birthday, it made her proud and happy. The fourteen-volume Goethe expensively bound would require a third bookcase from her landlady and would, with Leo's books, result in a very beautiful library. When they set up housekeeping together they would have to purchase a glassed-in case. *Set up housekeeping like ordinary people,* she wrote to Leo at the large desk in the furnished room where all her work with words took place. Bold sketches for a more humane society sometimes pouring from her pen, sometimes simply not workable. Yet *set up housekeeping like ordinary people* could have been a "Leitmotiv" of her life during the years of imprisonment and protective custody, with her love for people, animals, and plants and her lifelong dialog with poets, music, and painting.

No joy in motherhood, instead the desire to fight with her pen and for the time being instead of romantic holidays with Leo to snoop around the entire Leftist camp, little by little unsettle her adversaries and at the same time maintain contact with her Polish and Russian companions. An immoderate show of strength, which brought Frau Luxemburg high praise from the Party chiefs and some officials in the Reichstag for her brilliant work, until the illness that overtook her exhausted body compelled her to rest. Without her distant beloved, confessor, intimate, the mentor and critic Leo, who reacted to all her questions, demands, and war cries, she would not have had the strength either physically or emotionally for the exertions of her non-life. Zurich lay days away from Berlin by train, and the uncomfortable trips to meeting places in Germany were, despite successful appearances, more burden than glory.

In order to travel like a decent human being for two weeks in summer in Zurich with her heart's dearest, the vain young woman provided herself with a travel basket, where her things would not wrinkle as much as in a far too expensive suitcase. Besides that a large leather toilette kit and an umbrella; before she was able to depart Rosa L. had to put her books in storage and rent another place to live. The luxurious room with balcony and all her meals had become unlivable because of her muddleheaded, quarrelsome landlady. (...) *my landlady actually went into such a rage that I had to pack my things immediately and move out.* Once again on the move, without a room for the dear things awaiting her return, her life stations too transitory for a *Bobo*, the floor underfoot like a ship's planks, delivered up to the weather.

The group stubbornly defied the sharp northeast January wind on its way to Neu-Friedenau, which served a hundred years back as the center of the Polish Revolutionary Movement. Here in 1902 Rosa L. obtained her first apartment, where she would spend nine eventful years. A handsome middle-class house at 58 Cranachstrasse, and like houses at that time crowned with a little tower at the top. With a cozy balcony niche, a round oriel, a gabled stairway. On the fourth floor the red and the green bedroom-cum-study. Finally Leo Jogiches was installed as sub-tenant. The red room with Bordeaux tapestries and heavy velvet curtains, above the sofa a shelf for books, Amor and Psyche knickknacks, around the dining table upholstered chairs, several pictures by Rosa L., desk, bed, and washstand served as her personal realm. A toilet, no bath, the maidservant would have to sleep in the kitchen, and a houseman to beat the carpets. In the deep green room that was Leo's the glass case with books, desk, and armchair, wardrobe, and bed.

It is so clean in the rooms that in the sunlight one does not even see the customary motes of dancing dust that one can see almost everywhere. There is nothing to say, I gave our Anna exemplary training.

Had "Red Rosa" pasted together her political creed in the Bordeaux colored tapestries, fulfilled her life's wishes with her own household, an orderly existence? Then the present owners would not have had to protest about the commemorative plaque at the house for its famous occupant. But there it stands before the house, a parking place was removed to make space for it. The bronze tablet seems to have grown into the ground. The thorns of the rampant hedge roses refuse to allow dogs to soil the spot.

And we continue on in the double-decker bus. The microphone voice commented on Rosa L.'s Berlin years in outline fashion: her arrival, search for an apartment, the dogged efforts to acquire a local permit, her first appearance at SPD central headquarters on Red Island, a workers' quarter located between railroad lines, also where August Bebel lived. At bus speed we moved through the time stations. In the *Vorwärts* building the Party school, where Rosa L. became a Dozent in 1907. The steady income had made her financially independent at just the time of her estrangement from Leo Jogiches. The prison in Barnimstrasse is no longer there. The photo shows a long, gloomy building, its voices dispersed. So that we might view the structure from our seats the bus became one of the sightseeing monsters filled with tourists, whose heads turned as if on command in the same direction.

The last residential address, in Südende with her cat Mimi, I wanted to find by myself, more for the sake of continuity than expectantly. Locations wear down the slave to time, but not so her letters and writings, which appear inexhaustible, reaching out to later generations. Lenin is forgotten today, the Russian scientist in the bus remarked, but not Rosa Luxemburg. Lenin's mummified body a soulless shell, manipulator of the masses or a monstrance of the Party powers, given over now to the curious. Rosa L. decayed, became a plant, water, dust, but her burning words against the war and nationalism survived.

The bus turned into the street with the huge Springer buildings. As early as November 1918 this had been a media center, the microphone voice said, decisive for the revolutionary events of the Spartakists. Rosa L. had been freed from prison in Breslau, and after her talk at the cathedral plaza she had traveled to Berlin and went directly to the newspaper quarter. Her health from the long years of protective custody compromised, she had mobilized her last strength to write the daily text for the *Rote Fahne*. Despite her skepticism she had encouraged the war-weary masses with revolutionary slogans and had become a fugitive like her fellow fighters Paul Levi, Leo Jogiches, and Karl Liebknecht. An additional sixty-seven turbulent nights and days remained to Rosa L. until her murder. Too short a span of time to be able to make her political goals clearer to the public. And she suspected the end.

We are all held hostage to blind fate, what consoles me is the grim thought that I, too, will soon be called to the other side, perhaps by a bullet from the counter revolutionaries, who lie in wait everywhere.

She had taken action against the Social Democrat Ebert, who became Chancellor of the German Republic after the resignation of Kaiser Wilhelm II, and against his helper Scheidemann. Had fought with words instead of weapons in the knowledge that the time was not yet ripe for the fall of the new government.

Before the bus window the Prussian Parliament Building, another battleground of Rosa L. and Karl Liebknecht, the location of more defeat in December 1918. The Reich Congress of Worker and Soldier Advisors had taken place without her. At the founding meeting of the KPD by the Spartakists her counter suggestion, to name the Party "Socialist Party of Germany" or "Spartacus Union" had been outvoted.

And farther along on her path of passion. At each turn more agitation against the Spartakists and their leader, which would bring chaos and hunger instead of order and peace and a dictatorship as planned in Russia. Pogrom mood. Already in December the Freikorps and guard regiments faithful to the government came through the Brandenburger Tor, the city resembled an Army camp more and more. Eighty thousand Army members under Commander Noske against ten thousand Spartakists. The defeated troops of Flanders and the Argonne were to become victors over the Spartakists.

Her biographers have been diligent in recording events, including the ambiguity of Rosa L. herself. She knew that the revolutionary process within the German proletariat needed more time, she was for democratic rules and rejected acts of terror. On the other hand, her wrathful stand and smear slogans. She did not think of retreat, had felt it was a betrayal of the rebels, encouraged the rebellion of fighting workers who had lost sight of the outcome with leaflets and exhortations in the newspaper *Rote Fahne*. Fatalistic about defeat and ready for her own death.

Acheron has been set in motion, she wrote in November in the *Rote Fahne*. And later, in January 1919, to Clara Zetkin: *And in the end one must take history as it comes*. It was her last letter to her friend and political companion.

As fugitives Rosa L. and Karl Liebknecht finally took shelter with the Marcusson family in middle-class Wilmersdorf. On the walls of banners the invitation to denounce or murder, the price on each head one hundred thousand Reich Marks. Her small suitcase packed, Goethe's *Faust* and a few books included, a deathly exhausted Rosa L. awaited her bounty hunters. On the evening of 15 January 1919 men of the Wilmersdorf Citizens Defense Corps forced their way into her room and brought the defenseless woman to the headquarters of the Cavalry Guard Protective Division in the Hotel Eden, turned her over to a guard of murderous comrades. In the near vicinity of the Landwehrkanal.

The Rosa L. group gathered around the bronze tablet on the bank of the canal, which resembled a launching pad. In the lead-gray water the swiftly passing island of flowers could do nothing to ameliorate the graceless event of the murder night. About midnight the murdered woman was tipped over the railing of the Lichtensteinbrücke. One was able to observe the moving body conveniently, said a watchman at the hearing. He reported that Rosa L. had been thrown in the water and one could see her swimming, but the captain had not reacted. A tearless sky, a thick burial cloth above the field of violence.

A bloodbath that January with the dead in the hundreds. The dice had fallen, the show of strength so unequal between those faithful to the government and the rebels. With machine guns, bayonets, rifle butts the workers, Spartakists, and revolutionary soldiers were brought down. Doors were broken open and the defenseless dragged from their apartments and from the publishing houses and printing plants in which they were working. Even parliamentarians court martialed, hanged. Someone had to be the bloodhound, Commander Noske explained.

Rosa L. knew what threatened her. Her last text for the *Rote Fahne* lists the events of the previous days. Its title: "Order prevails in Berlin." She analyzed the political naiveté of the masses, the failure of their leader, and blamed the slaughter on the government.

Order prevails in Warsaw! Order prevails in Paris! Order prevails in Berlin!

The history of revolutions always ended with blood. Yet a hopeful Rosa L. swore there was a better future where the defeat of revolutionary battles would slowly but conclusively re-form into victory. It became her testament to posterity.

History, also, that many friends who outlived her died by violence. The first was Leo Jogiches. On the eleventh of March of the same year he was arrested, mistreated, and, scarcely identifiable any longer, shot in the head from behind and killed. History the abusive language like "old whore Rosa," to which she was exposed when she entered the Hotel Eden, the brutal blows of Hunter Runge's rifle butt at the side exit of the Hotel Eden which Dr. Karl Liebknecht, also arrested, endured and which later struck down Rosa L Unconscious after two such blows, she was dragged into the boot of an automobile that was supposed to bring her as well as a driver, side driver, hunter and another military person to the interrogation prison at Moabit. On the left running board a man with beard and monocle, Naval Lieutenant Hermann W. Souchon. After a stretch of one hundred meters he had drawn his pistol, which was still on safety, and held it to her left temple. And someone had shouted "Don't shoot." The Lieutenant cocked his weapon and fired. Her body still trembled afterward.

Perhaps you heard the click of the weapon, Róża. No one could swear that it was a lifeless body that was taken to the Lützow bank of the canal. No one can know what moved you in your last hours, what you thought about. The little limping Jewess who, threatened by a gray military mutineer, calmly climbed the hotel steps, sewed up the torn hem of her skirt in her room, and read *Faust* before her executioners came. Perhaps you fled into the other world of poetry, despite the threat wanted to remain human, as you had always remained human, as a politician, a prisoner, lover, as a committed theorist who thought in Utopian terms and fell out of reality.

Perhaps some seconds of dreaming were granted you, a kiss from the cat Mimi, scents of summer from Südende Feld or a time for love in the green room. Perhaps a blackbird sang its winter song, the walls became pervious and the room filled with people close to you, with the living and the dead. Perhaps the extravagant shriek of the wild goose on its flight to the south awakened a diffuse yearning. And life smiled at you, the actual life that you, a life-long traveler, sensed but it always seemed somewhere else and kept itself deliberately far from you, hidden behind one roof or another.

Or was the hatred around you stronger than the fantasy and you *so poor and abandoned like that God from Nazareth*, poor and abandoned, like the prisoner under protective custody on a Sunday in the fortress Wronke, delivered over to silence. Perhaps the unbridled noise of the soldiers reminded you of the wild rumble of the waterfall at Schaffhausen. Your anxiety at the train window that time before the white bubbling watery hell, your suspicion that the enemy was there. And yet you wanted *to plunge into the waterfall and go under like a nut shell* rather than submit blindly to what was happening.

You made the decision to sacrifice yourself and for a long time you have been practicing your farewells from beloved people, from the life plans set out for you. Time always pressing on you, granting you no idle moments, no time for quiet being on the sidelines as a researcher or artist, in harmony with everything that lives. And your knowledge of the inevitable, your worry not to be able to come close to attaining your political goals.

The light in your room at the Hotel Eden meager, your face within the circle of white hair like ivory, your entire person still as a statue, head buried in *Faust II*. Nourishment for your immense soul in the event your eyes were not too tired from the nights of working; and you stopped at individual sentences that you read to yourself as if they were psalms, but without making a sound. While Captain Pabst spoke by telephone with his superior Noske in order to confirm his final solution. A night without stars, without the wandering herds of clouds that you described with such astonishment.

Outside your door the watchman. You would not flee, have never evaded your responsibility, the concept of honor still taken seriously, lived, something that today sounds old and worn out was increasingly threadbare in the century of the wolves. For a long time you had distanced yourself from the *swamp frog society* of the Social Democrats, preferred to sit out the weeks in protective custody to their cowardly toadying, had long ago unlearned fear and until the very end you would show yourself to be fearless. That's why your opponent struck you with his gun butt. To strike down with brutality what she demanded, to break what they feared. Prisoners of their war ideologies, they needed the victim and believed they were buying a better future, a future soon to be threatened by the marching stride of Hitler's brown shirts.

Someone carried Rosa L.'s suitcase when, around midnight, she walked down the corridor of white lacquered doors behind which the civilian guests of the Hotel Eden silently waited. Closer to death with each step. A fragile woman in a velvet dress, with hat and gloves, a golden medallion her only jewelry. Upon leaving the hotel the two blows of the gun butt. When she fell someone dragged her unconscious body into the waiting car. The woman lost her left shoe in the process. Not far away, in the police station near the zoo, lay the murdered Karl Liebknecht.

Captain Waldemar Pabst, first staff officer of the Cavalry Guard Protective Division, awaited the return of the murderers: of Rosa Luxemburg it was Hermann W. Souchon, and of Karl Liebknecht, First Lieutenant Pflug-Hartung, The official report, with its account of events erroneously represented, had been quickly formulated. And it had been efficiently solemnized. Hunter Runge at the squad's dinner table, in the midst of his comrades, had passed a dainty lady's shoe, his trophy, from hand to hand.

Trophy, or better stated, relic, hardly qualified for shouts of jubilation, an indication that Runge's fellow squad members knew Rosa L. would never have need of her lost shoe.

But who finally took the shoe for himself, hid it possibly from sight, would be another story.

Perhaps it was a waitress, shocked by the noise of criminals, who did not want to believe what had happened on this night, remembered the charismatic Rosa L on the speakers' platform and wanted to perform a service of love. Perhaps the first person to weep for her was a chambermaid who entered the room lately occupied by Rosa L. and sobbed involuntarily, amazed by the strength of her emotional response.

One last time Leo Jogiches served as investigator, uncovered the murderous plot and made it public on 12 February in the *Rote Fahne*. He knew that the bounty hunters would not hesitate, that his life was played out. A few weeks later his capture and murder.

The seesawing politics of the military legal system and its all-too-casually functioning War Minister Jorns, a one-eyed legal obfuscator, would probably have analyzed Rosa L. gracelessly. Hermann W. Souchon, charged because of his disposal of a corpse and false report, was allowed to flee the country. The murderers of Karl Liebknecht were acquitted. It was May. And her body had not yet surfaced. Hunter Runge, obedient recipient of orders and super-sly farmer, had to spend more time behind bars than he had been promised in the chess game of arrests among the officers. When he threatened to become rebellious, began to talk too much, he was adjudged insane.

When a person dies, his world sinks out of sight and no one is able to revive it. Rosa L. loved life and every creature, staked her life on the reasonableness of human beings, non-violence, and she experienced fatal violence. Cain killed his brother, the human race remains hostile to each other. Was she ahead of her time or did she limp behind it, in any case it was the wrong time, a time in which her revolutionary ideas threatened the existing order. Thus she had to pay with her life earlier or later; who can know what the fate of the Jewish Communist from Poland would have been later.

When a person dies, a world sinks out of sight, leaving behind traces of things made with a brush or pencil. Rosa L.'s word traces tell of efforts to counter all the adversities in life with beauty. Her artistic language seduces, mirrors the intimacy of her letters and likewise the being of the writer. She sought dialog, argument, was fond of squandering her time and effort and for that reason, probably, did not keep a diary. Her letters breathe life, in no way outdated. And her *to be a human being (Mensch sein)* would still need to be redeemed by the coming generations.

But our present-day thoughts of profit focus on other values. The human being becomes exchangeable, an object that knows rivals, must depend on itself, with no solidarity. And Socialism is a coin taken out of circulation, although it still has value for the collector.

Perhaps it is her *to be a human being*, her identity of life and work, that draws people to her even now; and her life, which broke off violently, influenced nevertheless the history of the twentieth century.

An eagle, her antagonist W. I. Lenin wrote in 1922 in recognition of Rosa L., can indeed sometimes climb down lower than the hen, but a hen can never climb to such heights as an eagle.

He listed her political misjudgments: in the question of the independence of the Poles; in her assessment of more moderate Russian Socialism, 1903; in her theory of the accumulation of capital; her entering into negotiations for the union of the Bolsheviks with the moderate Russian Socialists, 1914; in her prison writings of 1918, which she rewrote for the most part once she was free again, in the last weeks of her life.

But despite all of these errors, Lenin concluded, she was and she remains an eagle.

His dependence on the well-known fable of Krylow and the listing of Rosa L.'s errors of judgment were a mixed compliment that coagulated into the canon of her critics.

5. The memorial tour bus reached Rosa Luxemburg Platz about noon. A billboard on the façade of the "Volksbühne" mentioned a Luxemburg performance. The bus personnel headed for the Karl Liebknecht Haus on the opposite side of the square, seemed to vanish in the chaotic crush through modest exhibit rooms, were found again in front of the house in the crowd, patiently waiting. The candy with the notation "In everyone's mouth" given out by the PDS as a scanty snack could not ease the effect of the icy wind that seemed to freeze one's blood.

I stood in the crowd, Róża, and was once again the child who stood in the crowd with her mother for a long wait. The same cold, the same surprised affect. The layer of newspaper under the child's shoes hardly isolated them, frost boils clung, and most of all the boredom, wedged motionless between sluggish adults, even her usual flight path into fantasy seemed obstructed. The railroad square bursting with people, a dark, faceless mass under kerchiefs and hats, shoulder to shoulder, closed in together. Let's leave the image there without sound, without the thunder of the fast train that could exorcise the ramp, the trains rolling out of the station, where someone named Hans waited for the human freight, sorted out suitable and unsuitable. And without the thunderous cries of recognition that bombarded the station, although not on this day. The lights in the windows like a solemn vanguard of firestorm nights in a total war.

The thin, cold-covered voices of the speakers in front of the Karl Liebknecht Haus were not yet finished, and in fact the two artists, a woman and a man, had not yet spoken. I had understood that the object under the cotton cloth was a life-size metal statue of Rosa Luxemburg. It was unveiled now to the applause of those present and showed a person standing upright in blouse and floor-length flowing skirt, well-formed hands, the left one closed. The line of a prominent nose cut the stern face, eyes gazed into the distance. Hair, the visible part of the back, and other body areas appeared to be incomplete, as if attacked by mold, as if some wild animal had been enraged, an animal or time itself.

A modest dedication ceremony, people driven off by the cold quickly moved away. I would come again, drawn by the person who seemed to me casually abandoned and unprotected in front of the undistinguished entrance. Most likely a provisional spot, but how much of the presence of Rosa L. endured today? The sculpture, like many other memorials, was made possible by private collection activities, came into being from many small contributions.

It was a windy morning when I sought out Rosa L again. No passers-by between the rows of occupied houses, the windows of the pubs blind, daily newspapers crammed behind a door handle as if their owners were absent for a long time. Rosa Luxemburg Platz was also empty except for the wind-blown puddles of rain. The single figure was separated by two or three steps from the sidewalk, a robust blue primrose at her feet, living protest to every frost.

I was on my way to the symposium of the Rosa Luxemburg Society that took place in the historically significant Bendler block, in a building blackened by time, with long windows across its front and behind it a courtyard.

A winter place where the powerful in residence changed along with the uniforms. After the murder of Rosa Luxemburg and Karl Liebknecht the Social Democrat Gustav Noske moved in as Reich Defense Minister. In the Second World War the high command of the army was stationed here. On 20 July 1944 the attempt by career officers on Hitler's life at the Führer's headquarters, Wolfsschanze, which failed. In that same night those taking part were executed, not far from the Landwehrkanal. The shots resounded, their brief pop, the silence stored in the walls of the Ehrenhof. Stauffenbergstrasse reminds us today of the Colonel, one of the chief conspirators. The historic rooms of the revolutionaries in the Bendler block became a memorial site: "German Resistance."

Opposite me at the long table the researchers, here from all parts of the world, who would give papers on "Rosa Luxemburg in International Discourse." Since 1973 these austere friends of Rosa L have carried on their joint international research, shed light on her life and her writing, and developed additional sources of inquiry. But is a Babylonian personality like Rosa L. to be read like a book or remain a mystery that, when it ends, cannot be solved.

The speakers reminded us of the lively circle of Social Ddemocrat committee members at the Kautsky family table, with August Bebel and the young Rosa L. Perhaps she would have smiled at the speaker who explained the political influence of Leo Jogiches on Rosa L. Many of Jogiches' best writings are included in her writing, Paul Fröhlich noted in 1939 in *Gedanke und Tat*. One cannot make a distinction between the two.

You know, don't you, that you are the only one, she wrote to Leo, *whose judgment I value, and who understands something of the situation.*

Perhaps she would have been surprised to know she was treasured in present-day Russia as a great humanist and fighter, and she would have joined in the lusty speeches and arguments of the Russians and the Poles. Perhaps it would have confused her to hear that imperialism, as she knew it, had probably led to ever newer dependencies; but over-production did not in any way lead to market collapse, instead it created new market possibilities. She would have reacted swiftly, in all likelihood, to the given situation and perhaps felt more at ease in the international circle than earlier in its political equivalent at the Kautskys. She wrote the following on a photo of Kautsky dedicated to his wife, Luise: *Eyes, facial expression—all excellent. (But the necktie, the necktie with the crawling white beans that literally fascinate the eye!)—Such a necktie is grounds for divorce ...)*

During the break a dense crowd in the provisional snack room, clouds of smoke above the confusion of voices, and then the other voices that call me into the rooms of the memorial site "German Resistance," into another time. On the walls a record of the trail of misery of countless human beings from whom the basic right of life was taken in the land of the master. As it was in Rosa L.'s time protective custody was also pronounced in the Third Reich. Her Spartacus letters are comparable to the flyers of the "White Rose," circulated by Sophie and Hans Scholl, which proclaimed passive resistance to all-out war. In February 1943 Sophie let the flyers rain down on the courtyard of the University of Munich and was, together with her brother, the author of the flyer Probst, and other students of the resistance group, sentenced to death.

They were young, like the "Skinheads" in black leather gear who shoved their way through the subway passages and, swaggering, compelled the late passengers to make room for them. How would they react to the name Scholl? And to the phenomenon Rosa L., which was not mentioned in the concluding podium discussion? In the subway I see with my mind's eye the image of a dump of a police station into which in September 1916 Rosa L had been moved from the women's prison on Barnimstrasse. Because she provoked an officlal, according to his complaint. Four weeks in a cell without light, squeezed in between a bucket for waste and an iron cot, the constant thunder of trains above her head. And she had declaimed Mörike.

My dream that night took me away from Berlin. I was surrounded by property owners. They demanded my person and the time that I had mortgaged long before and threatened me with damnation. Under pressure I asked for a postponement, had to be in Berlin next day, Berlin-Lichterfelde; didn't understand what had taken me away from Rosa L.

Sunday in a frosty light, the row of apartment houses unfriendly, quiet; the bumpy pavement gleaming, no traffic, only the diligent dog walkers cleaning out and cleaning up after their pets, the four-legged creatures obediently quiet this early morning. From the bakery the scent of fresh rolls, at the corner kiosk new news of the day. Soon customers would stand in line to buy bread and confide to the kiosk man the usual: that they would not cook today. Even women of retirement age would come, wouldn't they? Calmly the plump kiosk man handed out the pictorial paper, counted out the coins in their purse, and called out his customary "Bye bye."

In the subway isolated travelers, a man wearing a helmet, still wrapped in sleep, held his mountain bike. Without any transition the West face alternated with the East face of the city. The dark-skinned maintenance men in uniform whom I asked for information on subway connections mumbled unintelligibly and looked at me puzzled. They didn't know that the cemetery at Berlin-Friedrichsfelde became a pilgrimage destination every second Sunday in January for people of varying beliefs. Knew nothing of Rosa L. or Karl Liebknecht, the struggles for social justice. Perhaps they had been drawn into the caravan of the hundreds of thousands who, fed by people exiting the subway's cavernous holes, moved slowly forward spanning the street and pointed out the direction as if there were only one direction.

You were there, Róża, when I joined the caravan of women and men of every age who, with children, dogs, banners, and flags, walked on a path of carnations. No hand without a red carnation or a bouquet of carnations wrapped in cellophane, grew into an ocean of blossoms, and soon the red effusive rock with the inscription "The dead admonish us" foamed higher and higher around us. The orderly, solemn movement of the crowd was unusual and touched me, as if I were someone else in another time.

The thirteenth of June 1919, Rosa L. was buried in Friedrichsfelde, accompanied by thousands who quietly led the way carrying her image. On the banners the last sentence she wrote: *I am, I was, I will be.* Quotation from Freiligrath's poem, "Die Revolution." It had been a luminous early summer day with the chirping of birds, fresh grass, and the scent of blossoms, with newly acquired straw hats sitting flat, round, and stiff on the men's heads.

Heavy clouds of odor from hand-held bratwurst in the present, increasing the press of the crowds, two human streams—to the cemetery and from it. On both sides stands with one-liners from the fight songs of the leftist band, "Spektrum." A market place of ideologies, Róża, where I lost you for a while; where splinter groups with red flags and megaphones popped up to frighten the citizens, individual masked performers risking arrest, and Spartacus flyers on cheap paper that found no takers. A richly decorated bookstand enticed with long out-of-print works of great names exposed to the light of day and named Marx, Luxemburg, Engels, or Lenin.

Finally the wide gate through which the people moved, their long shadow, from which the shadow angel of carnations grew, impressive; shadow people who shoved their way slowly out of the zone of the dealers and into the shadowy place, accompanied by the music of Handel and Bach that sounded solemnly from black loudspeakers and made the people reverential. In various sized communal groups they moved patiently around the memorial site of the Socialists, name plates covered by red carnations, meeting no eye, no camera.

A place of unredeemed hope and of visions. The rebellion of 1989, the decisive outbreak of oppressed masses who brought down the Wall in the divided city without a show of force. On the banners of the civil rights workers one of Rosa L.'s main themes, that freedom is always the freedom of those who think differently. With the collapse of the Wall the dead of Friedrichsfelde, those who with visions of equality and a self-determined life objected to the official dogma, were no longer the property of the GDR and at the disposal of those in power.

But how much freedom does the human being need, how much can he endure? Rosa L. wrote about the growing political maturity of the ruled masses, about responsible choices in a Socialist democracy. Yet what is revealed is that the human being as a mass is still less capable of development than a political system and can hardly enjoy the freedoms he has. That he prefers barriers to uncertain terrain, lives his life according to pre-existing ideas, previous patterns, and dreams strange dreams. The malleable masses remain. Capable of seduction by individuals and their flags that point out the direction for them, "Hosanna," or "Crucify him." There is no need for war to have barbarism, no threat to one's life in order to be cannibalistic; boundless thoughts of profit is enough to dehumanize.

6. The brightly illuminated walls of the KadeWe beamed light out into the early darkness, the glass-enclosed passageways with their strolling crowds of eager shoppers seemed to sway, a unique bridge of sighs leading to a unique damnation: the palace of merchandise. Near each entrance, standing in the cold, the city's dregs, who demanded tribute from the consumers to keep from storming the palace. Anyway, they would achieve nothing if they went inside, would be

overwhelmed by the merchandise colossus, like anyone who innocently enters the labyrinth of luxury products. Shoved from floor to floor within the crowd of the consumption-hungry, who seemed to shrivel among the mountains of goods. Overspending to no avail, monopolized more and more by things, de-personalized. And then off to check out the rumor of a new shopping mall in wash-and-wear rayon, clouds of fragrance beneath which the addicted lingered, ate to excess with increasing hunger from the best to be had.

Rosa L. wrote to Mathilde Jacob in 1917 from the fortress Wronke that a package had arrived from the KadeWe.

I refused it.

A few streets away from the KadeWe the elephant gate, a strange sight with its pagoda roof, marks the entrance to the zoo, where a little troop of men and women gathered on this early evening in spite of the wet cold and probably also despite the keepers of the peace, who set up their observation post with four official cars on the Olof Palme Platz. Of no importance for the people waiting in little groups, who remained undisturbed as they chattered with what seemed like an old, well-established unity that knew a great deal about struggle but came here today with flowers. The square filled slowly. From the loudspeaker the powerful recorded voice of Wolf Biermann, which adroitly admonished and at the same time reminded one of performers paid to create the right mood at a political rally; but no favorite came into the arena here. Just a stately man who attracted my attention, white mane under a dark broad-brimmed felt hat, he towered over everyone. His long poplin coat hanging loose around his shoulders, he strolled among the groups of people, entering into conversations. Earlier he had stood out during the peaceful walk to the zoo. A lead wolf, he kept his eye on the pack, the older generation predominant. Tough old people who knew about bombing attacks, the "Economic Miracle," and wall-building, about airlifts, "cold war," the different kind of life in a divided city. Yet no one of those present appeared to have won anything with the Wall down, or was that not their intention? The casual laughter of an Indian woman whose missing teeth were corrected in the smile on an advertising billboard. A great city evening in shifting artificial light. From the loudspeaker the songs of Brecht and other Leftist classicists, as exotic as drums in a primeval forest. And also the Trotsky-like statements on politics and the world, on world police across the Atlantic, rather alienating, a Don Quixote sort of air without depth of feeling, which moved me simply because it seemed, in its nostalgic excesses, more human. A world invoked that was never a reality, only its advocates allowed to bloom. I felt like an outsider here and looked for Róża's face among the faces. Where would she stand?

The evening's course of events seemed rehearsed, tested, the prompt disman-
tling of the microphone, the quiet little troop that strode behind a small car that
filled the air with well-known songs and was itself led by a police wagon. Only
the dachshund wearing a rain cape and red scarf who barked violently at the
songs that attacked him from the open window of the car and the woman with
red socks holding his lead who did not stop him were surprising disturbance fac-
tors that no one heeded. Ignored by people on foot and others in vehicles the
group silently passed by a hotel where the Hotel Eden once stood. On the opposite side of the street a colorful play of lights and the sound of a marketplace
organ that resounded for a while.

It was the path to death that Rosa L. and Karl Liebknecht took and which
their faithful walked every year on the anniversary of their murder. They
approached the Landwehrkanal, its surface mirror-lit, the free-flowing grave into
which rain fell and punctured its surface. And again the rocking flower island on
the canal, including sunflowers, as if this were a summer festival. Perhaps someone began to sing, other voices joined in, perhaps for moments a glimmer of hope
before the long-drawn-out little troop turned in to the night-dark zoo, uniformed
men awaiting it who followed at a distance. Their official cars parked at the
entrance. Near their goal now, the women and men walked along an unlighted
path deeper into the lonely zoo without paying attention to the puddles. A biting
wind on both sides of the shadowy group of trees in the park and little glassy
lakes. Above the tall treetops a circling swarm of crows on the lookout for a tree
in which to sleep.

The car, that evening, on its way with Karl Liebknecht to interrogation in the
Moabit prison, made unfamiliar detours. The man severely injured from the
blows of a gun butt probably was unaware of it. And he would not bite the hand
again that had pummeled him with its fist. An evening like today, and the noise
of an automobile motor could come closer, occupied by a driver, someone in the
side seat, and the naval lieutenants, with hand grenades and pistols cocked, who
guarded the individual to whom they had shown the arsenal of weapons in order
to frighten him. As if the prisoner had a chance to escape his murderers, as if
everything were not already in play and incapable of being averted. Alongside the
Neuer See and farther into the unlighted side path where the auto stopped on the
pretext of a flat tire, and the somewhat unsteady individual was asked by his
guards whether he could still walk. Pressured by seven men with weapons in
front, to the side, and behind him he managed only a very few steps before the
first shot was fired, and Karl Liebknecht, killed from the front, plunged into

darkness. The flat tire seemed to be cleared up, and the murdered man could be given over to the emergency room personnel as an unknown dead person.

His Golgotha had been endured, and the fact of the prisoner's attempt to flee justified, although it was well known that Karl Liebknecht, like Rosa L. never evaded his responsibility. Both of them would be silenced this evening, a captain had already announced it when they had been brought to the Hotel Eden.

The rights of the lying militaristic accomplices in a wartime situation in the field were stronger than law and human rights, and the act of moving a corpse was not punishable. It was no coincidence that a long period of disintegration began with the malicious murders.

The voice of Karl Liebknecht was heard one last time in the issue of *Rote Fahne* for 15 January 1919, the day of the event. He believed idealistically in the distant goal of freedom for all in spite of the bloody defeat.

And whether or not we will still be alive ... our program will live, the world of redeemed humanity will prevail. In spite of everything!

The groups of trees were completely blackened by night as the women and men reached the spot where the murder took place on the bank of the lake and stopped near the Karl Liebknecht memorial. Perhaps there was something like a requiem, and someone tried to decipher the text on the plaque by the light of a match, finally read it aloud while more and more new match flames shot up. The lake was wind-crinkled, surrounded by gigantic trees, above them the firmament with one illuminating star that turned, seemingly hovering over this place, and, mirrored in the water, promised a special personal happiness through this special public showing.

The place was soon abandoned, the group had split into individuals who made their way in different directions. The police cars had moved off. The organ at the market fair still resounded through Budapeststrasse. Spartacus leaders Luxemburg and Liebknecht, born in the same year, were forty-eight years old when they were murdered.

A man in a yellow plastic uniform, a yellow umbrella open to protect his vendor's tray-cum-grill from the rain, enticed the passersby with steamy wurst, pressed mustard into rolls, and exchanged his product for cash. In the crowded subway an unemployed man unsuccessfully fought his way with a newspaper through the coach filled with the unemployed. Impatient youths with their long strides passed the weary travelers on the escalator at the last station.

Suddenly your smiling face, Róża, rose up at the top of the escalator, your face under a becoming broad-rimmed straw hat. Below that a serious white blouse with your string of pearls, the long tasseled shawl, its ends crossed over and loosely knotted, the little fold-over pocket, a decorative edging on the bodice of your dress. As if your person would grow towards me or I to her, as if someone who played an intimate role in my life awaited me in the humming wings of the metropolis curtain. A meeting about which I would gladly let myself be deceived. Reluctantly I separated myself from the image on the billboard, which promoted an event on the theme of "Rosa Luxemburg and Steglitz."

The apartment on Lindenstrasse was her last domicile and during the years of imprisonment a site of yearning for summer in Südende Feld, for the botanical gardens—closer to plants and animals than to human beings. Sometimes accompanied by Mimi, the cat with a past, who so impressed Lenin that he compared her to the stately cats in Siberia. Mimi, with whom one could tarry in the shade of the trees and who from time to time had a kiss coming to her in the event she was not in a grain field and cat-like ignoring the call to return.

I was absorbed in images, stories, as I crossed over Hermann Ehlers Platz, at my back the darkened Rathaus. In the center of the square a large wall of mirrors on which some two thousand names were written, birth dates and addresses of Jewish people. The announcement of the transport of the citizens of Steglitz listed children as well as old men and women, their names in the mirror retrievable, memory and admonition. During the day the market stands of dealers, a multitude of goods, the square alive with buyers, their fleeting images on the glass wall like the bit of sky, its fleeting clouds that Rosa L. would have described as disheveled, concentrated, bizarre, touched by their beauty, especially from behind bars.

Südende

7. The light holds promise of Spring. Brown catkins on the hazelnut shrub, woolly leaves on the bushes. Róża knew the botanical names, would have been able to tell me about coltsfoot, the red dead-nettle and the little white carnation stars in Südende Feld. About the smaller field flowers at the edge, *modest little creatures,* the early lily, on my way to Lindenstrasse, today Biberbacherweg. A side street, stately houses in large gardens, and Róża very far away. I did not ring the bell on any of the doors to inquire for house number 2, where Róża moved into five rooms with kitchen, bath, and large balcony.

An attic apartment on the third floor, a view of the broad flat land, at its edge the silhouette of the city, factory towers. Nearby the Teltower Canal and the movement of chugging tugboats, down two levels to the landing for passenger boats to Potsdam. Almost inaudible the rolling of trains, which reminded one of Róża's frequent travels. She had to exchange the quiet apartment with her cat Mimi much too often for long train trips. The rails like lines of time imprinted her political life.

Continually traveling. Agitated. Changing trains too often. Everything foreign, cold, uncomfortable. In foggy weather or African heat or in a windy rainstorm or she was jiggled in a horse-drawn cart from eleven at night to half past midnight. Many trips without lunch or dinner. And as always when she was on these trips to unknown places to arouse an audience she felt like a dog without its master.

My skull is cracking from weariness. But every evening I am fresh and talk for two hours.

The crush at her lectures burst the halls. Thousands stood in front of the doors, locked out. Ovations. Shouts for the speaker, at the end long periods of clapping and shrieking, tumultuous cheers. Twelve meetings in the month of her *visit to Saxony,* but it would be sheer impossibility to decline. She would have *to muddle through somehow,* hold on for these few weeks.

To hold on was a common chord for Rosa L., she always struck it as if for the first time. Equally powerful her yearning for the quiet corner where she could work and be, begin to live. Instead of continually turning out the day's texts

27

under time constraints and increasing her popularity through meetings. And, challenged by opponents, comrades, having to defend her singular position. Fighting instead of leisure. When her body reacted to the feverish work with pain and heart palpitations it was impatiently forced to do its duty. *But the strength, the strength it takes!*

So much strength for so much futility—or does futility need it? Does new strength grow out of it, an explosive strength? Was the rebel thinker kept behind bars for that reason and murdered a few weeks after her release? Did the energy field that could move masses of people have to be extinguished? The petite person in the black dress on the platform was neither witch nor Penthesilea. Her light voice filling the hall, her self-assured entrance, the imagery of her language were enough to win the people. After only minutes the hall was as quiet as a church. Perhaps it amused her when the opera glasses of the bourgeoisie were focused on her in 1902 in Cohn's banquet hall in the first Berlin parliamentary voting cycle. She talked about "social reform and social democracy," among the listeners many students, Russians, and Poles. Theater or circus ring, despite the certain applause, increasingly a battlefield. All around her the opera glasses, one after another; they could become pistol barrels directed at her person. At the world citizen without a homeland, who opposed imperialism and war and supported a mass strike in the German national military and police state, in public view under spotlights. It was foreseeable that in the Wilhelminian land of subjects, where obedience was regarded as a virtue, only a few wanted to follow the rebellious thinker on a long-term basis. Her Cassandra cries disturbed the well-preserved order. Whoever outlines a counter-world must be silenced. Pre-formed man resembles the snail, which carries its house on its back. Newness frightens, is a threat to it, a chaos. Before the masses make a move they need a turning point, some kind of debacle, a Waterloo. And yet no reformation, history tells us. And Rosa L. in the midst of it, her face overshadowed, covered by her own handwriting, rolled over by trains that transport her from meeting to meeting. To counter her fatigue aspirin and numerous cups of tea, and sometimes, too, a little Schnaps or a half bottle of Haut-Sauterne for one Mark ten, in order to endure her two or two-and-a-half hour talks. If the anonymous applause died away, she needed a trusted opponent who listened to her and answered, even if only in a letter. A bridge of words that carried her and her friends. From all the rooms she occupied on her journeys her exacting reports to Leo, later to her boyish lover, Kostja. What was not to be attained became language, an instrument on which no string was left untouched.

A quiet day at her desk in Südende, where Rosa L. worked on *Die Akkumulation des Kapitals* and Mimi purred on the velvet armchair opposite her. A happy day that she depicted, like so much of her life, in letters. The white hyacinth. The crystal prism. A paperweight on the table in the sun.

… sprays of rainbow by the dozen spread out from it onto all the walls and ceiling, and it was so colorful and cheerful in the room.

Her life was similarly multihued. As a politician and the first female lecturer at the Party's School of Economics and National Economy. As a war opponent who spent four years behind bars in protective custody. As an intellectual, for whom literature and music were as necessary as breathing, who painted and studied botany, who was a researcher. As a female human being who wanted to live life to its fullest. Quite extravagant for the one short life, too little leisure. Perhaps the long enforced pauses behind bars were more exhausting than her high-flying time. But the eagle was too strong for a life on the sidelines. And if she were to endure it, she'd limp herself raw.

Back to the calm streets of Südende. The apartment houses like stage sets placed in the grass and videotaped momentarily. Then if a bus stopped on the one-way street women with heavy shopping bags would set off in different directions, disappear behind solid doors. Towards evening automobiles, one by one, would roll into open garages, soon lamps and TV screens would light up the happiness in the square.

I'd better let the scene run backwards. Instead of houses, garden plots, and instead of arcades the view over Südende Feld. On her balcony a crowd of raucous sparrows feeding and Mimi, who chattered angrily. The limping *cripple-sparrow* had no chance. And then, too, crowing was to be heard, twittering, outcries, trills. Seasonally there was blooming or there was snow; then the temperature of her rooms fell more than ten degrees. Despite that, the cheerful cold shower around six and nudity in the fresh air of her bedroom. The lonely walk through the snowy streets late at night, the sky a night blue.

And sometimes the desire to *air out something*. With her servant, Ida, in the Steglitz Cinematograph Theater, at 30 pennies for a seat in front, among servants, children, and messenger boys, emotional stories with music that made her and Ida cry. But all at once her laughter, which astonished Ida.

Many different affairs, all in a pouring rain, as it always seems to be. An evening that amused Rosa L. very much. And as usual her pointed report on the day to the "you" of her letter. A trail of words from her desk, from her cell, or from the travels that reflect her life.

8. The correspondence with Leo Jogiches was comparable to a long novel of a marriage. At the beginning the man in the leading role, the stern advisor, sup-

porter to whom the woman listened. The beloved, with whom she wanted to share everything. Professional work and partnership. Money and good taste

Do you have any idea how much I love you?

He loved her too, his extraordinary partner, knew that her journalistic pen and her charisma were an ideal enhancement to his revolutionary work. They were like-minded, but their temperament and their goals were too different for a life together. Long hesitation before following the woman from Zurich to Berlin. Was he fearful of her astonishing successes or for his own independence? His Sphinx-like attitude made the woman impatient, his reluctance and the pleasure he took in criticizing her produced lively mixed signals. She described her success as a speaker, her role in the Party elite, the social occasions, and her wardrobe. Reported what she was working on and what she read, covered her lonely Sundays with writing. Wrote letters and texts, fervent in heat or cold, described for her distant beloved a life that exhausted but at the same time emancipated her; remained accessible to him, however.

She still saw herself as the wife of the reddish-blond quiet revolutionary and fantasized a life together, while he seemed perfectly satisfied with epistolary embraces and kisses on his *Bussi*, held her romantic feelings in check. The extraordinary woman wanted an ordinary household with the extraordinary man, even an eagle needs its eyrie. And then the pressure from her family, for whom she invented her engagement, followed later by a wedding celebration in faraway Switzerland. Why should she expect her family to take on more truth than the latter could bear, that she was called Frau Dr. Rosa Lübeck on paper only, and the dissolution of the fake marriage was put off. Mademoiselle Léon, as the man's family affectionately called her, bowed to the prevailing rules of her time. The man, who reluctantly followed her to Berlin in the summer of 1900, was introduced to her Party friends as a Polish comrade.

Finally her own ménage was in place, with a girl named Anna, Ida, or Gertrud, and the Frau Doctor and her melancholy boarder. A rabbit that hopped through the red and green rooms was added to the family. Later the woman would live most happily among animals, and the cat Mimi would take the place of a child in her life. Mimi's behavior, her moods, her digestive system, Mimi's greetings and kisses would play an important role in her letters.

For the woman a life with the partner who shared her love and struggle was still imaginable. At the same time she continued to gain influence as an unimpeachable politician and brilliant writer. She opposed the arms race of the great powers and the revisionists in her Party and had already published significant writings, for example, "Sozialreform oder Revolution?" The opera glasses were always aimed at the dark-haired woman with the fiery eyes when she strode onto the international political stage, elegant and confident of victory; dined with the Party elite; enjoyed an evening of theater, a concert, or opera. The man avoided the public, a gray eminence who gradually fell into the role of secretary to the woman.

A conspirator in retirement, he saw to the best train connections, kept track of her appearances like an accountant, was advisor as well as critic, otherwise remained a phantom. His influence was indirect. He was a leading figure in the Polish Social Democratic Party of the Kingdom of Poland and publisher of Polish journals that he smuggled illegally into the country. The woman molded him, wanted to shape him, perhaps, whenever she outlined a better way of life or corrected his wardrobe, but she always continued to court him.

Please … no thick and hairy material, that is provincial. Take a thin, soft English material, very dark gray.… But the coat black and broad-shouldered, well cut, the way I like it.

Everything was good, she wrote from away, she behaved herself admirably, all according to his instructions; he ought to be quite satisfied with her. Word bridges instead of a life together, from her to him to her, when for months at a time he accompanied his deathly ill brother to Algiers and she traveled to meetings in halls filled to overflowing. Her reputation preceded her everywhere, she wrote. In Crimmitschau, where more women than men had come, a woman was the first one to speak in the discussion that followed her talk. Everything went wonderfully well, she wrote most often. Her fine for insulting the Prussian Minister of Culture seemed not to upset her.

In August 1904 she would continue to correspond from Cell 7 in the prison at Zwickau, mostly with her *little blonde one*. The man was to provide her with a warmer blouse, in an *unattractive* color, and the smallest size stockings. She described the day's activities in her cell, annoyed at his ascetic life, which she saw as lunacy and abnormal. She took note of all the sounds outside, the measured tread of horses' hooves on the pavement, animal voices, a waltz played on a harmonica. And decided to live life to the full when free again. There was time to read Schiller and reflect long and hard on the Polish mess of her inner life and to work with more determination on her writing. She ignored the stomach problems caused by a prison diet. And if the man worried in an all-too-patronizing manner, his sentiments were rejected in her next letter. Perhaps she felt his worry was nothing more than a substitute for love.

On the occasion of the coronation of King Friedrich August of Saxony the woman was given an early release despite her protest, and everyone would have granted her and the man a little private time. Life as a couple, and the servant Anna to manage the household. Conversations around the green lamp, evenings with a small group of friends, a peaceful life with her pen at the side of the man. It remained imaginary.

As a matter of fact, it is a wretched fate, she wrote years earlier, *that as far as our personal life goes, something always gets in the way.*

Instead of an idyllic time: in 1905 the drum roll of the Russian Revolution, which sent the revolutionary to Warsaw in order to continue on site his underground war for the Polish proletariat. Again the bridge of words that connected their lives, the epistolary dialog, the woman's war texts for the common political front, her admonitions, kisses, and his meager confidences about what was happening. Time ran against them. After his short visit in November it would be years before the man saw the green room again. The woman would remain bound to him until death, but much would be different. Her long hope for a quiet happiness finally torn to shreds like the large articles of laundry caught up in heavy winds in the garden of Südende. It had sounded like the chatter of enemy gunfire.

9. On the Treptower Canal numerous Borsalino hats without their owners float downstream, look like uprooted water plants. The soundless demonstration a dream in the night. Above the wintry roofs the morning star. I would soon ride through the empty streets of Steglitz and be a traveler like Róża.

The harsh east wind on the railway platform sent travelers fleeing into the small glassed-in waiting area. A multinational flock forced to crowd one against the other in the close confines: the snoring bum beside his morning ration of empty beer cans; the youth in a wheelchair, which necessitated shoving our luggage to one side. The over-long legs of the black man, which caused new arrivals to stumble, or the rippling words of women in kerchiefs near the tourist with a backpack who regularly dug out his Coke to take a noisy swallow. The breath of the waiting group fogged the glass walls and made the thunder of the trains more threatening, as if the sound would become a solid mass, roll over everything and drag it away. On top of that the loudspeaker voice, a puzzle of word fragments, as if it concerned news for travelers who had arrived long before.

The train that entered Berlin in May 1898 had run over a man at midnight and had to spend a quarter of an hour on an unused track. Awakened, she had heard a human scream. It had been a farmer who wanted to drive his oxen across the railway embankment in the dark. To her question whether the man was alive, someone answered: ... *just a little bit.* That was not a god omen, she wrote to her own Leo.

Suddenly the bum awoke with a start and, as if in a panic, wove through the waiting room making boxing thrusts. I utilized the possibility and managed to get to the exit behind him with my luggage. From the loudspeaker the report that my train would be fifteen minutes late because of an accident.

Warsaw

10. The city in which the seven-member family Luksenburg took an apartment and the little Róża would spend her childhood and school years is no longer there. Countless steps resound through the Rundbogen Tor, noises, knocking, hammering of residents of the building behind the garden, poor salesmen who under Czar Alexander III led a frugal life. Tall Antoni, too, is an image from yesterday. In the early morning, summer and winter, he propped his face and hands on his broom handle at the pump in the large courtyard, unwashed and brooding, in a short sheepskin jacket. And the little girl, who crept to the window in the morning quiet to look at life, although it was strictly forbidden to get up before her father. And abruptly Antoni's loud, unrestrained yawn as he started his work with the wet broom, almost playfully cleaning the stony courtyard.

I hear even now the shuffling, slapping sound ... The way he swept the courtyard, it was a poetic act.

At eighteen Róża would no longer be satisfied with the view, would apply for a passport, leave the city, the country, and become a student in Zurich. As a member of the underground movement "Proletariat II," she had come under suspicion. It is said that the revolutionary M. Kasprzak helped to smuggle her out of the country. Concealed within a covered wagon and with the help of a Catholic priest who supposedly helped a Jewish soul to convert. Perhaps only a pretty legend, because Polish universities remained closed to female students. The intelligent, ambitious Róża did not want to wait, like her older sister, for a possible husband. She wagered on more knowledge, an independent life.

In the Second World War Hitler's occupation forces turned the city into a stone desert. The Baroque palaces, churches, classical merchant houses, the ghetto, the Renaissance houses in the Old City quarter, the monstrous prison structures of the Pawiak were bombed or blown up before they retreated. The mighty sand and rubble cone from which individual walls towered with blind holes that were once windows, was a dead place. Its people were necessarily resettled, became displaced foreign workers, exploited independent of their age. Became less than human beings with no rights, and in the concentration camps strewn over the country 5,900 were murdered.

The face of the city reconstructed was another face, and many of the historic buildings that were rebuilt in the style of the eighteenth and nineteenth century became even more beautiful. Like the splendid Renaissance houses of that time around the Old City marketplace. Their residents no longer have to scoop water from the municipal fountain like the impoverished laborers in Róża's childhood. But colossal structures and faceless apartment silos on the outskirts of the city of two million remind one of the long postwar period of Socialism. Only the Weichsel imperturbably moves toward the ocean, indifferent to the changing scenery of time and in Danzig Bay combines with the Baltic.

However, it was Róża's city and her history in this city that I wanted to retrace. That is, the history of the Social Democrat Anna Matschke of Berlin, who on the 28th of December 1905 as the correspondent of *Vorwärts* took the train for Warsaw and was accompanied to the Friedrichstrasse railway station by all the Kautskys. She wore a wool plaid because of the cold and a blue loden cape. Luise K. slipped into her pocket a jeweled watch with the initials R. L., *dearest Lulu.*

A cold light-less day on which Rosa L. as Anna Matschke departed, and the train took a long detour through East Prussia because of insurgents. *All night long … dawdling here and there, am tired as a dog.*

At the Illowo station schnitzel with potato. And continuing on in an unheated and unlighted train with a complement of soldiers, finally reaching Warsaw, which she had left sixteen years before, on the night of 29 December.

The snow-wrapped city was deathly calm, as if the winter freeze had taken hold of the people, too, who lived in fear of the Czarist secret police Ochrana and the soldiers. Every day arrests and threatening gunshots. Every day two or three people stabbed in the street by soldiers. The Russian Revolution had spread to Russian-annexed Poland, the authorities reacted to the general strike of the oppressed Poles by declaring a state of emergency.

After seven years of intensive but theoretical work in Germany, Rosa L. wanted to prove herself on the revolutionary front. She would publish the underground paper *Sztandar* along with Leo Jogiches, who, as Otto Engelmann and correspondent for the *Leipziger Volkszeitung*, had slipped in from Austrian Krakau. He would continue his Party work in the illegal SDKPil at the same time. Rosa L. took a room in the boarding house of Countess Walewska under the name Anna Matschke.

11. The small Polish Airlines plane dipped lower. Travelers in business suits emptied their last vodka in anticipation of the coming weekend. It was an effortless

flight over country borders, over the land of Polish rulers, its forests, acres, lakes, effortless and transitory. Flowing images, flowing time, on the way to places that know about Róża. Perhaps my coming here would be a success, perhaps I would lag behind and not be identical with the traveler who, before she climbed into a taxi, had been warned she had to wait for the guide with the mini-bus.

First impressions through the car window. Broad veins for traffic traverse the city space, new office towers seem to be everywhere, the chunky structures of the '50s era frightening. The tradition-rich hotel near the Old City that existed in Rosa L.'s time was destroyed in the Second World War. Rebuilt, the house resembles an old lady who keeps up the plush style of her youth, only tolerates the best materials, but wears fake pearls and plays the coquette in blue jeans. Marble stairways in Bordeaux red with decorative iron balustrades faced in brass are mirror images of each other. Dark leather sedate club trimmings in the large lobby compete with blue plastic columns in the bluish-green restaurant with plastic food that was taken back again indifferently. Plastic world peopled with artificial figures, a new generation of self-conscious makers and do-ers who illustrate their market value clothed in the latest style and accompanied by a like-minded and -clothed lady friend. In the rooms the clear admonition to keep the window closed in one's absence or at night, to lock the doors, secure the safety chain, and secure valuables in the hotel vault.

Sauntering along the streets I told myself that I was in Poland's capital. It seemed as if there lay between the city and me a no-man's land, I needed time to conquer the distance between us. The light unreal, filled the city as if it were still Indian summer and southern birds were not already in winter quarters on the Nile. People on their usual Saturday stroll. Music somewhere and squat kiosks, a crowd around a magician. From a megaphone words snaked endlessly, breathlessly, transfixing onlookers to the spot. And I understood that it was a tussle for voters, the song of the rat catcher still bewitching.

I chose the opposite direction. The Sigismundsäule near the king's castle and the Old City was besieged by young people. With Coke in hand and the sound of transistors in their ears they stretched out in the late light like cats, threw long shadows along the square's pavement. Catlike, too, the woman with a camera who continually prowled among them, filming their young faces. As backdrop the city walls with the Marschallturm battlements of another time.

Baroque and Gothic churches to be reconnoitered and in each its faithful, who reverently took part in the Catholic Mass. Kneeling before the priest the main characters in festive white and black, as if a wedding were possible only on this day, and the golden light would promise special happiness. Each time I left the scene quietly. Did the young Róża take her idea of child and marriage from the city of her childhood?

In the narrow Old City alleyways a southerly push of people, tourists mixed in. Gift boutiques and galleries still invitingly open, and in the circle of the Old City marketplace restaurants enticed with al fresco dining. Above the tables a darkening sky, glimmering stars, the coachmen's departure theatrical. They sat rigidly on the box and perhaps calculated their take while the horses steered them toward their stall, hoofs clattering in unison. In a gallery bright with lights a last stubborn shopper. She resembled the woman with the camera, the same determined face, the same easy movements. I named her "Cat." A gentle scent of hemp rippled around the Sigismundsäule, stimulated the boulevard as if this were a metropolis. A full bus in front of the hotel ready to take its cargo to a piano concert in Chopin's birthplace. A travel guide crossed off the names of the last tourists to board. Through the revolving door of the hotel on the other side of the street the rhythmic beat of a mazurka sparkled, soon drowned out by the shrill siren of a police car. The anonymous faces of the prisoners behind bars.

12. Rosa L., the revolutionary, felt good in Warsaw as Anna Matschke, better than in Berlin, where she cursed *all this God-damned politics* in a letter to Leo, the *idiotic duty to Baal.* Wrote that she was close to letting go of this bloody parody of a political life that they both led.

Far from her Party fathers she resembled a young woman who has finally freed herself from family pressures and can live with heart and reason in the full force of her passion. Without the adaptable tactics of the SPD functionaries, against which she rebelled, and against the politics in the old order's leisurely progress. Instead action, a mass strike against the miserable social circumstances in Poland, the Russianizing of the country and the avalanche-like unemployment. Students and intellectuals had joined Polish workers, but when Anna M. appeared in wintry Warsaw the Czarist counter-offensive was already underway and the wave of strikes in check. But better a life of strife, exposing the army's raids, the spies who, infiltrated in factories and revolutionary cells, did their Judas service, than to continue muffled in the listless climate of Berlin. Her fiery lifestyle needed a spark, and again she set out to enlighten the masses who, once brought into motion, would be able to free themselves.

Perhaps she had already met Leo Jogiches on the night of her arrival. Or it was a polar cold morning when she walked the short stretch from the Countess Walewska's boarding house to the Hotel Victoria and asked to see Otto Engelmann. Perhaps the snow crunched under her feet and reminded her of early winter paths to school, the daily exertion of covering up her limp. The limp was always more noticeable when she was tired, but she was not tired, not yet, looked forward to her underground activity with Leo, who proved to be nicely German as Otto Engelmann.

It had been a difficult year for their union, the Revolution and his secretive small-mindedness, as if he consciously wanted to exclude her. But he expected her letters and texts on a daily basis, these *newspaper smear campaigns*, no matter how beset she was with other work. How was she supposed to be able to work without his information about what was happening at the site of the action?

To run around head over heels on a smear campaign, I know how to do that very well, but to know what it is all about, I don't want to have anything to do with that. It's an old story, anyway.

But now she was here, and in a few days it would be a new year. And the love affair with Witold was over. Leo had made that necessary, *laissez faire, Goldchen*, why talk about it any more, she never liked to do that. She lived the life of a plant, and he would have to let her be as she was. Her sister Anna L. had sent her a light blue blouse that she wanted to wear on New Year's Eve and perhaps, indeed, why not? a new blue velvet skirt. Her income from *Vorwärts* made her independent and left both of them in really good financial condition. She would never be able to accept his *hollow-cheeked Nazareth posturing*, but this was not the time for private conflicts, their common passion for the Revolution was stronger than the mutual alienation.

Although he behaved properly at their first meeting, it could not please him that she had pushed her way into his war zone and with her important acquaintances and unmistakable appearance endangered herself and all of them. They worked together each day, and it seemed that with their camouflage names of Anna and Otto they had gained some distance from their history as a pair and could meet without restraint. Otto, the experienced tactician, was dangerously incautious when he took a room near Anna in Countess Walewska's boarding-house. But perhaps they needed to be near each other, to have the illusion of safety. And to succeed for moments in forgetting that the general strike had failed and they were now counted among the hunted minority. The Damocles sword of imprisonment, the threatened execution of those captured was constantly above them and their comrades. There were difficulties in producing the *Rote Fahne* on a regular basis and to disseminate it on the street. In the middle-class printing plant revolvers had to be held on the printers to compel them to print until a house-to-house search was threatened, and a government seal brought the printery to a standstill. Another had to be found.

Despite everything the work continues cheerfully, she wrote to the Kautskys. *After all, ... no one is injured. And already today a new printery is as good as captured.*

She appeared to have strength at her disposal that astonished her. Produced with robotic precision topical articles, pamphlets, flyers, fluctuated intellectually between an armed revolt of the proletariat and democratic maxims. And she believed persistently in a long-term change in the power structures, dissolved by an altered class consciousness, the rebellion of the masses.

When Anna rode through Warsaw in a sledge to the weekly meeting with her siblings, she was aware of her exhaustion, and she experienced it oddly enough with happiness, felt it intoxicating, like the waltz that time into the twentieth century with Goldchen. Or was it the thrill of playing with risks. She did not know if she was being watched and with her visits to the Luksenburgs her identity as Anna Matschke became questionable. Her sister and her three brothers would have liked to see her more frequently, had no suspicion how unsparingly she exploited her brain and body. It seemed as if she mastered her work in a trance, like a fakir who runs over the glowing coals barefooted without burning the soles of his feet. In revolutionary Warsaw she lived more intensively, vehemently. Perhaps one needs more danger in order to treasure life.

Time resembled passenger trains rolling past, a fleeting impression, even the sixty-five days of hectic togetherness. One spring-like Sunday, the fourth of March 1906, Anna and Otto spent the evening in her room; perhaps they embraced. Anna prepared for her return to Berlin and had her visa already in her purse. She would never use it. Instead, on the evening before her thirty-fifth birthday she and Otto Engelmann were arrested by the Russian secret police and provisionally locked up in the jailhouse near the parliament building. Perhaps in saying goodbye to each other they took quiet courage in the knowledge that their cover names would not protect them for long, or no more time was left for them, everything was spent. They did not suspect that the forceful separation would change their lives and lead to the end of their love relationship.

13. The bright silver Volvo stood in the hotel lobby as if fallen from the sky. A chandelier threw points of light on its spotless skin. Doors and trunk, invitingly open, were reflected in the marble floor. Resembled wings that could lift the metal animal. Its many admirers respectful, as if it were more than an article for sale, a museum piece from the capitalist West and not attainable. Somewhat to one side a graceful woman in tiger leggings, leather, elegant stiletto boots. "Cat"

again and her camera eye. She filmed the scene persistently and seemed just as scenic with her red cap of hair, her powdered face, her supple movements.

Rosa sometimes accompanied friends *with a car* to Lake Schlachten or into the Grunewald and felt the increasingly noisy traffic while she worked a disturbance. Aleks, my driver, knew little about Rosa L., but a Polish lighting company carried her name. As a cosmopolitan Marxist who placed herself in opposition to Polish nationalism, she was always a controversial figure. Now in a Poland once again Western-oriented and democratized, she was a person who did not fit anywhere.

But hadn't she written a much noticed doctoral dissertation about Poland and its industrial development? And while still a student composed her furtive exchange of letters among prisoners for the independence of Poland? And didn't she go to Upper Silesia on her first political agitation trip? Had Rosa L. become a German through her fake marriage or had she always remained a Pole? She felt newly born, Rosa L. wrote to Leo as an election campaign traveler in June 1898, enthused over grain fields, meadows, forests, the breadth of the country. Enthused over the Polish farmers, their language, the local air, that she could not get enough of hearing, smelling. Poland remained the country that she inhabited with her heart and for which she gave her strengths as politician and writer, imposed on herself an increasingly harsh life, time against her.

Aleks, a polite law student who accompanied me, soon understood that I preferred the Pawiak and the citadel to the famous Königsweg. And I was a tourist of the ashen paths that led me to the fortress Wronke and a prison facility in Breslau. It was during the command of General M., head of the Polish prison system, that the walls would be made impervious for hours, walls behind which Rosa L., the opponent of war, spent twenty-eight months in protective custody during the First World War.

But did I need to see the authentic place in order to know Rosa L. better? Wasn't everything already expressed in her letters and writings? My reconnaissance resembled the behavior of a sightseeing pilgrim searching for an urn with the dead heart of Frédéric Chopin in Holy Cross Church and who was more affected by the experience than all the preludes and nocturnes.

Or was I searching for more than that, to continue the Polish-German history of Rosa L. that concerned me as well. As I approached her images of another time were crowding into my memory. The little knot of a dog from Galicia, for example, who came home on furlough from the grimness of the campaign and collapsed into the sleeping child's bed, or the night the bombs fell and the little Galician in the south-German city licked his burns.

Pawiak and the citadel are historical memorials today. Both gigantic prisons came into being in the nineteenth century under the rule of the Czars. Places of suffering and resistance known to Rosa L. as she grew up, which remained hidden in her like the forbidden writings of the poet Adam Mickiewicz.

Probably it was for that reason that the thirty-five-year-old revolutionary found her arrest in the boardinghouse Walewska stimulating rather than a shock, although the single cell provided for the fourteen politicians was unreasonably crowded.

Now we all sleep like kings on wooden bunks diagonally set up, beside each other like herrings, and everything is going really well.

In addition, there were the attacks of the crazies, the constant quarreling of the mean element. The cells stood open all day, the prisoners were able to move about through the corridors, had to endure the prostitutes' quotes and little songs, the open door of the toilet and its odors.

Maybe she felt ennobled, an equal now of the many political people who had inhabited the cells before her time. Youths, proud women and men who died during the transport of prisoners to Siberia or over the bumpy cobblestone pavement of the long death street, through the death gate of the citadel, led to their execution. Her friend Kasprzak was among them, had been hanged a year before her arrest.

She knew that the situation was serious when, after five days, she was unmasked as Rosa L. and transferred from Pawiak prison into Pavilion X of the Warsaw citadel before the gates of the city. That because of inimical conspiracy there was a threat of martial law, by which she could possibly be exiled to Siberia. But she took it calmly and wrote to the Kautskys quoting Goethe's Faust: *We live in turbulent times where everything that exists is worth dying for.* And as usual she wrote topical texts that even made it out of the cell and into print, utilized the quieter night hours until two in the morning.

The lengthy sprawl of the Pawiak structure was mined and destroyed by the German occupation forces. The Pawiak prison museum stands on what was then a field of rubble. A place heavy with history, even now, raised from the rubble by former prisoners with their own hands. Pieces of wall, door hinges, bars to prevent forgetting. And again the image of a woman forces its way through, a woman who carefully rescued a small iron from the ruins; pleased with her find, she showed it to her child. That same year, 1944, the population of Warsaw began to rebel against the German oppressors. After sixty-three days of bloody resistance the city was reduced to a stony wasteland, the survivors driven out, shipped out, murdered.

The stones know about it. The voice of those in pain in the bricks of the Pawiak, inaudible to the visitor who slowly walked through one of its corridors. On each side the austerely outfitted cells, with iron fittings on doors to secure them. A peephole for inspections. The barred window in the corner directly under the overhanging vaulting prohibited any view outside. Above the cell door names of prominent inmates and the length of their imprisonment during the Czars' reign. Human remains spilled onto sand by the wave of time, carried forward.

The two-headed Russian eagle, characteristic symbol of Czarism, on the wall of the interrogation room, replaced by the Polish eagle between the First and Second World War. And then the swastika. During the time of the Hitler occupation a hundred thousand prisoners in the Pawiak. Daily interrogations and torture, the transports into death, to the execution locations around Warsaw, into the annihilation camps.

Cars with megaphones as messengers of death drove through the city, Róża, the right of humans to life was set aside by non-humans. During the four-year occupation 700,000 Warsaw residents lost their life. But there was resistance. Creativity opposing the fear of death. Underground resistance and retaliation.

The maternal attendant seemed the last prisoner in the dismal Pawiak and was glad to enter into a conversation with Aleks. She dug around in a locker and found a Polish brochure on the rotating history of Pawiak Prison. Beside the name of members of the forbidden SDKPiL the name Róża Luksenburg.

It is again 1906. Prisoner 317 was photographed in her coat, registered, and secured in one of the cells in the three-story women's prison, Serbia. On a yellowed photo the lengthy structure, a one-story guardhouse, in front of the tall gate made of iron rods a cluster of waiting people who knew relatives behind the walls. Locked in or locked out was all the same here, the oppressors' fear made itself known in the size of their prison building, the restricted autonomy of the oppressed.

No watchtowers as we left the area, the huge gate all that remains of its pillars, Róża, and out from them protruded a massive horizontal iron rod, covered with iron spikes and bulges of barbed wire, like a gallows tree or a totem pole. Not far from this skeleton of a tree a memorial tree with a tablet of names that stood for the countless numbers of nameless sacrifices, and on the horizon the building blocks of the new time.

Aleks took the ashen path to the ghetto, shoving his car between the tourist buses. A no place. Just a quotation with a memorial, the street of memories, the memorial wall in place of the tracks onto which the trains rolled with their human freight for Treblinka. Aleks indicated a fallow flat terrain that held remnants of the wall surrounding the destroyed ghetto and that people wanted to leave free before a silo would cover everything like a grave marker, silencing the stone witnesses.

The 500,000 ghetto inhabitants, treated like human merchandise, sorted according to their usefulness and misused, had shrunk to 60,000 when the resistance broke out in April 1943. Young Jewish women risked their life serving as couriers between the guarded ghetto and the city and smuggled the weapons inside. After four weeks of resistance a deathly calm over the ruins.

And I thought of the girl Róża, who at Christmas 1881 experienced her first Jewish pogrom, thought of her dark fear. Three days and nights the ominous noises raging through Zlotastrasse, which was not in the Jewish quarter. Broken windows, boot heels striking doors; there were injured and dead, and the Czarist police did not intervene against the pogrom.

Yet Rosa L. wrote to a friend in 1917 from the fortress Wronke, *What is it you want with your special Jewish pain?* She knew the pain of the Jews, but she knew as well the suffering of the blacks in Africa, whose bodies were used by Europeans to play catch. She knew the pain of all the oppressed. So many screams reverberating unheard would sound in her that she had no special corner in her heart for the ghetto. She felt at home in the whole world, where there were clouds and birds and human tears.

14. At my back the shimmering band of water that was the Weichsel. And up the hill that was to be climbed the citadel, like a voracious man-eating stone animal resting above the river since the time of Czar Nicholas I, consuming, as it protected the ramparts, what was supplied to it. On the terraces the silent witness of crosses, arranged in stiff rows, detailed for a parade of their dead.

Generations of political prisoners were quartered in Pavilion X. Nearby the gallows, close to the nut tree at the wall; in the courtyard of the barracks the waiting *kibitka*, a gloomy crate on wheels to transport forced laborers to Siberia.

With her transfer into Pavilion X of the citadel in April 1906 confinement conditions for the prisoner Rosa L. became more stringent. She could no longer contact political friends as she had done in the women's prison of the Pawiak. Could not receive letters and flowers or direct writings to the outside world. The flight plans of her helpers were also made impossible. Judgments based on martial law were threatened and her Polish and German comrades were justifiably concerned. Together they exhausted all possibilities to protect the native Pole with a German passport from forced labor.

A single-story barracks surrounded by small houses with nameplates, the cannon's barrel set up in a soldierly manner, ready for action. And near the ground-level barred window with the Arabic number ten one of the small houses painted in zebra stripes. Perhaps Rosa L. could hear the wake-up call. White hairs shimmered in the prisoner's otherwise dark hair. Strong eyebrows emphasized the velvety-dark but steady gaze in face-to-face encounters. But the oval face with the stern nose and mouth had grown pinched. Doctors' findings at the end of May, made possible by her Polish comrades with a gift of money, confirmed her anemia, a nerve condition, distended liver, and an abdominal-bowel catarrh. After a six-day hunger strike she could only manage the walk to the visitor's room on the arm of the fortress commandant. Meeting her siblings was nightmarish. The weakened Rosa L. had held herself up with both hands on the wire grille of a cage that stood in a larger cage and thus resembled a wild animal in the zoo. Looking through the mesh of the doubled cage in a dark corner the siblings had scarcely been able to make her out. Her brother tried to examine her face with his face up against the mesh grille, but tears would have clouded his gaze again and again.

Alarmed, Jozef and Maksymilian contributed to the feverish efforts to free their sister. For the medical attestation of her condition 2,000 rubles, for the master of the guard 3,000 rubles bail as well as her promise not to leave the city opened the jail doors on the 28th of June 1906. The weakened revolutionary with a yellow tint to her skin continued to be observed but seemed, as sickly as she was, no danger to the Czaristic system.

Despite her ill health, her fighting spirit hungered for work. She knew that she had changed and burned to disseminate her experiences in revolutionary Warsaw to the German Socialists. The *latest quarrel* between the Party leaders and the workers amused her from afar and was for her like dead mice giving birth or very dead insects, while she here in Warsaw was having a splendid time. A time that brought masses of problems, gigantic crimes, gigantic embarrassments, gigantic stupidities, and it pleased her to sketch a pretty picture of all these giganticisms, especially in *Neue Zeit*.

The revolution is grand, everything else is senseless!

Her fiery temperament needed conflict and action; she accepted the risks. She lived above speech, excluded no color in her effort to reach people, her friends, opponents, and the anonymous masses to whom she accorded more maturity than the reform-oriented Social Democrats.

The visits to various authorities that she was compelled to make through the summer streets of Warsaw were taxing, as was the uncertainty when she could leave the city to spend some time at a foreign spa. After an additional medical attestation Rosa L. was allowed to travel outside the country to a spa, but her foremost goal was Petersburg, where she sought advice from political friends. Using a cover name she sought out her old friend Parvus in the Peter-Paul Fortress and narrowly escaped arrest. With guards at her neck, *the little beggars*, she reached the nearby Finnish town of Kuokkala and using a false name took quarters there in the villa of a painter. Here, too, she met with Petersburg Bolsheviks and with Lenin, her key theme the Revolution and how to continue. Did the future lie in the present?

Rosa L. recovered in the summer bright villa. In a few weeks she wrote her great essay, "Massenstreik, Partei und Gewerkschaften." She succeeded in showing that, with respect to the multi-peopled kingdom of the Czar, revolutions were not a governmental event, not something to be planned like the city on the Neva under Peter the Great, but rather that they came into being as the proletariat rebelled against its enslavement. And that the restless parrying of smaller groups, like the demand of industry workers for an eight-hour-day and more rights, could become an extensive fire. The Petersburg workers who went to the Czar's palace in January 1905 had a peaceful intent, requested help in their misery, and died in a bloodbath, triggered more revolutionary actions.

She thought often of Leo, who was sitting—his identity discovered—in a Warsaw prison, threatened with a Siberian work camp. She exerted all the more rage in her writing, reviewed all the newspapers of the previous months, corresponded with German Party friends and traveled to Petersburg to cheer up friends in prison before their imminent deportation. She seemed a different person when she walked through Petersburg's colorful streets, without anxiety for herself. It was as if the Revolution had strengthened her and imparted a commission to which she gave her whole being. In her letters from Koukkala there is no summer poetizing, no clouds or the bird calls that formerly figured in Rosa L.'s correspondence. Her mind was laden with fighting voices, and she had fallen out of love. She returned to Germany the end of September another woman.

15. The long drawn-out death street of the citadel lay completely empty in the afternoon light, on the wind the lamenting bim-bam of a bell. At that time it tolled before every execution, usually in the first hours of the morning. No one knew for whom the bell tolled, whether it was his death bell, his cell door would noisily open, and he would have to begin his last walk surrounded by guards. The waiting was a martyrdom, a pre-death, as if breathing would come to a standstill, and everything that was his identity would be lost forever. And then the footfalls in the corridors, the clinking of chains that slowly moved off, the echo of the

shots. Then the hands that knocked on the walls and brought them to speech would conduct the death report from cell to cell, all in Pavilion X, and no command of the guards could choke off the sound. They had already suffered too much.

The bell still ringing, my head a bell chamber, and every stroke a pain. On the huge memorial tablet of dark marble were the names of all the prisoners, but I sought and did not find you, Róża, they had updated the tablet sometime ago, Aleks told me, and Róża Luksenburg was no longer included. But what was is not eliminated, it buries itself in time and forms its own history.

Heavy traffic in both directions along narrow Zlotastrasse, no possibility to stop the crate of a car at Number 16 and get out. Quick glances from the car window. The girl with long dark hair and a fringe of bangs wears a school apron and could be on her way to the girls' high school on Wilcastrasse. The two Schnauzer-bearded policemen in Russian uniform on patrol come swaggering towards her and force the girl against the wall. The wall gives way and closes behind her. At the corner a hurdy-gurdy man is playing for the children. This multinational colorful Warsaw in the glow of its Russian masters had, like the girl and her school, disappeared.

The roast duck on my plate was a realization of the postcard image in the window of the new old restaurant in the walled-in square. You will eat the best duck here, Aleks assured me, a national dish instead of a hamburger, but for the farmers things were in a bad way, a pretty sight to see them simmering. His own grandfather had chased the court executor off his property with a manure fork. Under the Red regime the interest rate for credit had been less than the price increase. The interest rates of the present economy would lead to forced auctions. But the farmers went on the defensive in spite of clubs and tear gas, even the miners, steelworkers, doctors. The history of Poland was a history of the underdog and his revolt. Since the opening to the west Berlin had been approachable; on weekends the Germans would come to the other side of the Oder, populate the forests and lakes and buy up old estate land.

Did he feel threatened by this, I asked, and he studied the dessert card silently, looked out the window. His eyes, blue or green or something in between, reflective.

He made do, Aleks said, but he asked himself if that evil spirit that had twice caused a world war were not like an underground water source that, unnoticed, works its way upward again. Its force increases, and the stronger wins. For that reason he was studying the law. After passing his qualifying exams, no mean feat in Poland, he and a few friends had built a fire on the shore of the Weichsel and celebrated. Suddenly out of the darkness a band of "Kibice" with knives and chains had attacked them, and his friend Andrzej, with the grant of funds for his mathematics study already assured, was bludgeoned and thrown into the water like a dead cat.

And I understood why he did not react to my suggestion, today, that we stop by the river but instead increased his speed, so that we were in an area so densely constructed on the flat land that apartments like beehives mounted into towers, with little eating establishments, uninviting shops; and that we then followed a long wall. Behind it the other city, Powazki, its metal crosses, cupolas, mausoleums, bronze statuary protected by old trees. Aleks stopped the car in a parking area near the main gate, said he would be back soon, and disappeared. I slipped my card with the same information under the windshield wiper.

It was November-quiet in the space for the dead, only the whisper of the leaves in the avenue, which seemed to lead straight into endlessness, but with many branching roads that were not to be overlooked. Just as manifold the headstones, fantasy art forms of their designers. The size of the monument corresponded to the fame of the one resting here, and often a weathered little bench was set beside it, anchored with chains. Many a gravesite already fallen in, nothing to see in the earthy space. A leaf swayed loosely from a tree and stopped moving, as if held by an invisible thread, or was it a mirage. Suddenly a hand took my arm and the imploring voice of an older woman, a mishmash of Polish and German underscored with gestures. I understood that my leather backpack could easily be taken from me by thieves and went to the exit, where Aleks waited. Had he sought his dead friend?

His dessert fork fell clattering onto the stone floor and broke the silence at our table. And the set guide-time had run out.

There was still light on the fortification "Barbakana," a strange contrast that left the walls sparkling and the grass in the moat colored an artificial green. The young people whiling away the time on the low wall in little groups that continually changed places left me thinking of more southern regions.

The woman sitting tailor-fashion on the wall let nothing disturb her. She wrote so hurriedly in a book that she might have been following a fast dictation, and I recognized in her the red-haired film person in tiger leggings whom I named "Cat." She was so immersed in what she was doing that she seemed not to notice that I looked on, craving the words, and envied her racing pencil. Beside her was a bottle with green contents, and a baguette rose lance-like out of her over-large purse. I would have liked to photograph the still-life with the writing woman, although I never use a camera.

Anyhow, the moment had passed. She closed the book, and I could just see the handwritten title, "Mary Winn," before it disappeared into her purse. Nonchalantly she swung her legs and smiled when she noticed my glance at her bottle. It was an herb liqueur, she said, in a Swiss-flavored German, would I like to try it? She removed the cup from the top of the bottle as she spoke, poured, and handed me the cup. It tasted surprisingly bitter. Cat drank from the bottle. She then said that her name was Mary, and she had gone to Ireland to recover from problems in her love life. She tore a piece from the baguette, spread it with a smoked Krakauer and began to bite into it with obvious pleasure while she told the story of a hammock that sounded like a love story. The young people had long been just phantoms. Picturesque the phosphorescent points from their smoking, and we walked towards the lights.

Cat did not know what I sought in Warsaw, knew nothing of Róża. Perhaps we would meet again, everything was open, hovering like her story of the hammock. I don't drink liqueur, but this evening in the hotel bar I looked for the bottle with the poison-green contents.

The weathered stones protecting the base of the maple tree had grown into the earth like old men, only the chiseled script in Hebrew and the number of years seemed to withstand time.

A dream on this night where I believed I heard other voices besides the sound of the rain. Perhaps those of Eliasz and Lina Luksenburg or Róża's siblings. Were they resting here from their life? I made my way deeper between the trees and the disheveled stones lying about, which also could be the lost teeth of a giant, wanted only to escape the place and the cold wetness. The little roofed-over stone hut stood across my way, open at the front like a dollhouse. Strewn over the ground the flickering of multiple islands of candles that projected the shadows of two women on the wall. Hair piled high, long dresses, wasp-waisted. I turned around, but nothing was there, and the lights were soon extinguished.

I awakened to the rustle of rain, which reminded me of my dream, and I wished myself back, planned how to make the two women talk. The bright silver Volvo in the foyer and its admirers, all just like yesterday, the feverish guests at the desk. Only Cat nowhere. A vigorous rain crackled down from a leaden sky, and no one seemed disturbed by it.

Aleks in a post-war rubber coat drove to the central railroad station while he explained about the homeless, who would settle for years in there. It was known throughout the country that the administration was watching. With time the railroad station had sunken to an asylum for bums, and then a falsely understood outreach organization saw fit to offer help with showering and cooking. People lying on benches, waiting rooms gone to seed, finally compulsory eviction, and the protest camp in the railroad hall.

Under the roof of the railroad giant the restless pulse of the traveler, carrying his own luggage. Arrivals, departures, standing in line for tickets. And like an island the others, who had fallen out of time. Their possessions laid out around them, they chatted or took a first swallow from the bottle or slept rolled up in a blanket, unconcerned with what went on around their camp. The red-white national flag set up between them and those traveling through like a border tree. A quiet but impressive demonstration of broken down existences, they were like professional city pranksters who wanted to remain in Warsaw until the city fulfilled their demand for rent-free dwellings.

Was it a threat or a despairing attempt to make themselves noticeable, and would the travelers soon have to pay a discreet passage toll in order to reach their train on time? The siege reminded me a little of the well-known play in which an honest man admits arsonists into an attic room in his home as guests and finally even provides the match for the blaze.

And how would Rosa L. see the campground of human flotsam and jetsam in the railroad hall, the uprooted Polish Jewess who even as a schoolgirl experienced social inequality. Probably for that reason resorted to Marx and Engels and in a cell of the forbidden party "Proletariat II" conspired against the Czarist exploiters, became an inevitable rebel.

Aleks admonished me again never to leave my luggage unsupervised and disappeared.

Berlin

16. Jackowice, Kutno, Kolo, Konin, place names that passed by like the broad fog-soft country, the pine forests, black and white flecked cattle, groupings of birch, small bodies of water, and grazing animals with shaggy hair, flocks of crows on fields whose crops had already been harvested, straw-covered houses; from concrete-gray clumps of apartment buildings topped with a confusion of antennae, to industrial chimneys, Coke or McDonald's signs removed, and—without transition—the flat country again, bright pumpkins, hand-turned tree sculptures, asters, a last poppy.

Sometimes the two calm Polish women who sat across from me, wrapped in coats and scarves, smiled. The train was still unheated and the older of the two shook with attacks of coughing from time to time. I shoved over to her a packet of sugar-free herbal cough drops and felt taken up into her company. The clatter of the refreshment cart and its offerings, the same everywhere. The women served themselves and encouraged me, and I understood that all the provisions were included in the fare. Suddenly the train slowed and stopped abruptly, as did the restless cups and saucers on the little folding table.

The long avenue of poplars moved straight along to the unsecured railroad overpass, the red warning light unnecessary. The street was empty, as if it were no longer in use. At the edge of this image a shadow, phantoms popped up, soon recognizable as a small cart and horse that swiftly approached. Two men were in it, their weapons shouldered, their booty of wild hare proudly guarded by a terrier. The glazed eyes of the hare knew no heaven.

17. In times past, she remembers, the little Galician dog had the task of retrieving the *Völkischer Beobachter* for Rehn, on furlough in the uniform of the German Post Office East. And remembers the glass-eyed fox fur from Poland's forests, the spoiled Christmas goose, the meat poisoning, the hand-made lace coverlet for the marriage bed. The stories about trips within his district to the post boxes in the occupied country. About clouds of dust and farmers' one-room houses where the life of the extended family and their animals played itself out between the hearth and the bed. About Polish hospitality, ripe cherries from the tree, the helpfulness

of the Polish Post Office workers, whose work protected them for some time before they were displaced. About partisans and higher wages for dangerous work, frozen dead bodies on the gallows, vodka evenings in the Post Office head-quarters and a secret deal with the owner of a gold-rimmed oil painting before the latter had to climb into the truck.

The little dog, Sarras, came from a pack chased under a train. The hand-made lace coverlet was bombed along with the apartment. The oil painting of an alder tree a useless object without a wall, as useless as the initial pilgrimage to a bomb crater at the outskirts of the city, the greedy rummaging for bomb splinters as souvenirs. The child liked the garden dwarfs and wheels that turned in the wind in the little front garden, but not pilgrimages, open-air markets, processions, mil-itary festivities. If there was a threat of such an event she hung her apron on the handle of the living room door, left it open a little, and hid.

18. Podstolice, Kostrzyn, rain pearled on the window. The dark heads of the wil-lows like stony sculptures on the tear-drenched land, its inhabitants resettled, eth-nically cleansed, swept away. All these dreadful station names seemed to her like so many stations of the suffering of human lives, Rosa L. wrote in January 1907 to her boy lover Kostja from a dreary second-class waiting room. Why were there actually so many cities in the world. And why would people simply bring so many children into the world, did Kostja know how to explain it?

The wheels rolling, coupling complaining, the chance community of travelers as it was then, Róża, nothing else as it was then. Water seeks its way to the ocean, trees continue to root, but the people were shoved like goods through the conti-nent. Driven out to stay in the houses of others who had been driven out of their homes and—resettled somewhere—preserved their homes and towns in their heads, the place where they knew their dead. When memory goes with age, who will tell of life's customs, its needs, the epoch of world war, the human caravans and their murderous drovers. Who will tell to prevent forgetting?

The melodious voices of the Polish women enlivened the compartment and seemed to me as intimate as the rain land outside the window. As if there were remembered stories older than I that would answer the voices of the women.

Perhaps mother and daughter, the younger wheat-blonde, jeans under the short coat, with stylish little boots, embodiment of the new Pole. She would offer me a cigarette in the corridor of the train and tell me about her studies in English at Posen. The feet of the older woman were fitted into brown pumps, and her eyes knew of the war.

The noble republic of Poland was divided, torn apart, at the end of the eighteenth century into *the three black eagles*: Prussia, Russia, Austria. In spite of bloody rebellions Poland remained until the end of the First World War dependent on the three states. "The Tragedy of Poland is its geography." (Max Frisch)

The train pushed on through the earlier Great Poland, a territory that was under the administration of Prussia and that Rosa L. often traversed as an election speaker. And where she was taken into protective custody in the Fortress Wronke during the war. The massive clinker structures behind the massive wall remain witness to Prussia's dictatorship and serve until today as a prison.

A barred railroad car, from which the prisoner Rosa L. saw the landscape, the small railroad stations, places as if on a screen move past in October 1916. And perhaps the sky was heavy with rain, as it is today. The settlements seemingly strewn in the distance, a wet dog chained to his hut stands statue-like at his post, an occasional church tower. The pastoral office probably lodged for a long time at the site of power in the city; at that time or today clouds of prayer in the cathedrals and the hope of those turned inward to be heard, their faith a strategy for immortality.

My journey through the land of Róża's birth seemed to me like a journey through numerous time zones. In each place I came closer to the time when she lived there. And the images of my time became mere dots that shoved themselves in between, attempting to continue to tell her story.

19. Rosa L., on her way from Finnish Koukkala to Berlin, wrote at a table in a railroad hall that began to rock to and fro along with the floor and walls and reminded her of the journey by ship: sixteen hours through the turbulent sea, to and fro until she didn't know if it was Sunday or Monday in Stockholm. And it really shoved her forward, too restless for long epistles to friends whom she would soon meet. Her next station was Hamburg, where her paper, "Massenstreik, Partei und Gewerkschaft" was published. Then Berlin, where the Kautsky family would be waiting on the platform for her arrival as they had done when she departed. And on to a Party rally in Mannheim.

September 1906, when Rosa L. returned, rebellious ideas for the hesitant Party people in her luggage. She had risked her life at the revolutionary front, which she felt was her happiest time. Impressed by the Poles' will to fight, spurred on, she felt herself called to carry the spark onward. Instead of parliamentarian straws the rebellion, her creed for mass strike. The strong SPD could not expect that the Revolution would fall from the sky; when would the Party fathers learn from the Russian Revolution? And understand that the misery of the mine workers, the railroad workers, and the factory workers was to be fought only by means of a general strike. A people's movement could not emerge from the Party central committee but had to arise spontaneously from the masses, whom one must enlighten and encourage.

By God, the Revolution is great and strong, may social democracy not kill it.

Rosa L. was still regarded as a revolutionary who had just come from there, but her model of a mass strike did not suit Wilhelminian Germany, where the SPD philistines strove for more seats in the parliament. She had placed herself on the opposite side and distanced herself from the theoreticians of her Party. Her analysis, "Massentreik, Partei und Gewerkschaft," was rejected by the union as too radical and squashed with the approval of the Party. Her German passport had not made her German among Germans. She felt the changed climate, her increasing isolation in the political arena and suspected that in the event of a war the German Socialists would defend national interests. As an internationalist, comfortable in several languages, thinking in national categories was foreign to her; however she was also a believer and single-minded when she prepared her talks to the public and understood the applause of the audience as the agreement of the majority for her revolutionary slogans.

Perhaps the rocking railroad hall anticipated the coming movements. In December of the same year Rosa L. was punished by the Weimar government with two months in prison for agitating the public. Before that, a southern trip to Maderno on Lake Garda with Luise Kautsky.

Never was parting from the south so difficult, she wrote in the train back over the Brenner Pass. *Every jolt of the train, every winding of the tracks away from the south cut me to the heart.*

The new year began with the sentencing of Leo Jogiches by the Warsaw military courts to eight years of forced labor in Siberia and a lifelong banishment from the region. The absent Rosa L. was declared his accomplice.

In Germany the election campaign for a mandate in the parliament. And Rosa L. was again on the road as the best speaker. But whenever she left the speaker's platform she felt empty, monopolized by the anonymous masses, which she understood as an abstract entity that she wanted to move, but whose proximity she endured with poor grace.

Was she less a radical than an intellectual with a romantic impact and only incidentally still caught up in the political machinery? And in the wake of the revolution had her old yearning for happiness in a corner of her own been activated? There is no answer, only supposition that she wanted to bail out of everything. And in her life that, with the pendulum of time swung out in this direction or that, the heart side never forgot. In the later "pistol years" when her attack mode only triggered enmity and she would feel more and more isolated, the heart side, a faded *Liebestraum*, could have played a part. She would strangle herself with her soldierly decision to exert more severity, clarity, and modesty in her life. She fought with just as much iron will against her political opponents and the Party leaders. Would attack the Party line of the fathers in her writings and talks. Quarrel with Lenin. And snub the Party leaders with her slogans for mass strike and military disobedience in the patriotic pre-war period. Would therefore be gagged and lose influence with the forum in the large Party papers.

For the time being out of the fire of the revolution and into the red and green room, carefully kept in order for her and Leo, a refuge. But Leo awaited transport to Siberia in the vile Warsaw Mokotowo prison. In the green room young Kostja Zetkin, son of her Stuttgart friend Clara, who took up residence there during her long absence and was looked after by the Kautskys. When she returned she was agreeable to the situation. In any event she was usually away, and when she returned there was a gentle man who revered and admired her, in the end not a man of action, one who loved nature and long walks as she did and with mountain climbing forgot his mother's instructions to work regularly. She would soon manage to reveal the world to the "baby," "prince," "Bubi," "little tiny sunbeam," "heart's sparrow," guard him from the smallest pain in order to know that he was happy.

She sat at her desk in the red room lost in thought, a velvety fringed shawl around her shoulders, her dark flood of hair piled high on her head, her eyes gently happy. Her hands lay on the pages of the open book as if they would feel a story with their ten fingers. A secret love story in which an extraordinary woman chooses a man-child. Wants to shape the child as his maternal confidante, lover, and advisor. Who would understand better what to read in him, to advance his talents. She will let him sound out his living space but give him cues. A puzzle from which an image would form that she already saw completed in her mind's eye. For his formal education he would have to read a great deal, the son, read into texts in the original languages and also learn to understand Russian, because life bubbled there and one drew one's breath there more easily than in the suffocating air of sleepy Germany. She will see to getting books for him, suggest titles, search indiscriminately all through the intellectual landscape. Stendhal or Dostoyevsky, Tolstoy, Balzac, the Utopians, philosophers, and naturally Engels and Marx. He could begin with the national economy and study history or become a writer. Why not a writer or artist? She would read the same books, they would exchange ideas about them, their paths of thought would meet.

A photograph shows *Little Ninunius, my sweet lover* beside her on her winter balcony. Taller than she but youthfully shy, he gazes downward while she looks confidently into the eye of the camera. Everything appears to be other than with Leo. The thoughtful young man with a dark crop of hair and dark eyes had courted her, and she listened to him, ennobled by their love. Were they not both outlaws of the classical norm? Romantic souls who dreamed together but did not publicly live together. Circumstances kept them separated more than together. The many hundreds of letters tell the story, a thread of yearning words which she spun around herself like a cocoon, perhaps more dream than reality.

It doesn't matter, it was a time of love. And she was in love with love, which caresses all the senses, in a glow of love, which makes people and the world more beautiful. It doesn't matter who caused the feeling, it was intoxicating, like a fairy-tale. Finally a luminous chord, the teamwork of bodies, mind, and soul. Her fantasies multicolored in sound, a round dance through Arcadia.

Her talk enticed, courted the love object with poetic images that love fed into her. Or she reached for a sketching pencil and immortalized *Duduk* in sketches, the youth with the heavy head, *a Renaissance figure*. In knickers and loose shirt, easily dissuaded from study, or reading or relaxed on the disheveled bed. No servant, no visitor to disturb them. Only the twosomeness of the artist and her model. Her observant eyes on his muscular body, the serious face that her sure hand happily re-created. Perhaps she sat in her dark green robe of ribbed velvet, entirely given up to her muses, and her model let himself become gently bored, not wanting to escape his mistress. As a child she had gazed at a rosebud all day long and hoped in vain that it would bloom. It happened at night. Would she experience the young man's development with him, or would she have to go away unexpectedly, leaving the yearning behind?

She continued to sketch her beloved *Duduk* on paper. With his back to the observer, his round head buried in the crook of his arm, his body outstretched except for one leg oddly bent, tensed, as if his foot were practicing running away. And one day, who knows, not only the foot, and then she would have only his image, her *Duduk,* on paper. Her easy panic. While she completed the image it occurred to her that the distance between them would increase and he would in the process become smaller, indeed disappear entirely, and not be embraceable any more.

She continued to puzzle over her love's time, dreamed with her "heart's sparrow" about traveling south. Travel out to Corsica, for example. For once stroll around with her lover with no rigidly prepared rules of caution, in a silken dress from Paris and with the blue hat. His new grey suit, mass-produced, elegant yellow shoes. But she was also careful to consider that she would go into a mountain hut with him; when he wrote about it she would be able to breathe his mountain air.

Instead of that the speaker's podium, the parliament elections at which her party lost half its mandate. Her lonely fight against the colonial politics of the government, the increasing nationalism of the man in the street, against imperialism, the threatening danger of war.

But happily Leo Jogiches had escaped from the Mokotow Prison, she reported to her young man at the Stuttgart house of his mother. He had disappeared in Warsaw and would probably be in Berlin soon.

His green room, like her love, was given away. Instead of Leo everything significant was shared with the twenty-two-year-old Kostja, he was to comment on her work; the vacillating, helpless youth was to take over Leo's advisory role. His judgment, his embraces, were indispensable to her.

The dawdler, a gentle boy upon whom the fireworks of her talents, wishes, sudden ideas crackled so that he childishly marveled, with no notion that he was the cause and should gradually conform to her expectations. The little one willingly let himself be guided; they exchanged maps for meeting points. Cards or life geographies. Imagination replaced reality, which was too much for him. Her feelings for him became all the more vehement, her anxiety about him, the anxiety of loss when he ran off after a speech, disappeared into the crowd and she could not see him any more. Why didn't he wait for her, was he dissatisfied with her?

The woman on fire had succumbed to the youth's admiration or love. Elixir and compensation for her life of work and fighting. The love object, more chance than a stroke of fate, had come to her, had to be similar to the image of her love. She took up pencil and oils and began to illustrate her irrepressible yearning, feverishly, as long as it lasted, until the color dried and the illustration was able to be mailed, only happy when he praised her. She thought herself loved, courted love, was sparkling with youth herself and extravagant. Or sad, heavy with migraine, suffering when she remained without echo, and the glow of the moon hurt her eyes. Compelled herself, however, at the same time, to do her duty; subordinated the privacy of their passion to her life as a politician who had to follow her convictions.

Perhaps it was evening when Leo came. The servant opened the door and let him enter. He who had escaped banishment did not suspect that he would be banished again, and none of his strategies prevented him from it. He unbuttoned his grey bouclé coat, which was lightly sprinkled as was his full beard, reminiscent of winter snowflakes that had been caught in the rough weave of his coat and in his hair. But it was Spring, the linden trees would bloom and Rosa L. would travel to the meeting of the Russian Worker's Party in London as the delegate of the SPD and representative of Poland. Leo Jogiches would take part in the meeting as a Polish delegate, certain that their political work like their life together would be continued.

Perhaps he sat with Rosa L. in the red room and they cautiously circled around the time of both their imprisonments. Thirteen months, in only a few of which Leo was free but constantly in danger of being recognized before he escaped over the green border. A Polish comrade had taken him in. It was possible that she became his lover during that time, and Rosa L. forced that confession from him. Possible, too, that he discovered love notes from Kostja. Leo had lost not only his green room. He was a decisive fighter, his deep bright eyes could grasp a situation with lightning speed and would react rashly. A two-year war of attrition began. Lie in wait, enrage with words, spy on each other, threaten. To oppose his threatening hand on the revolver the woman would protect herself with a Browning.

It was not a good journey to London for both delegates, the complaining voices of the buoys on the sea voyage reminded the woman of death bells. Aspirin for her migraine. But then the gloomy Metro, endless stations to the part of the city with which she was unfamiliar. The murky flicker of the lanterns mirrored in rain puddles, the garishly colored restaurants and bars like a stage backdrop and in between the nocturnal scene of newspaper boys, flower girls, drunks, noise, shrieks, the crack of a whip, a pre-Hell perhaps, oppressive for the delicate woman who made a wrong turn on the way to her hotel and asked herself why she had set out again on a maelstrom of a life instead of pursuing her yearning for an island.

Yet soon another string began to vibrate and she had a desire to dip into the over-foaming metropolis night and be carried along in it, to escape her strenuous life for hours and sample all the pleasures. She overheard couples through the thin walls of her room, their laughter, shrieks, saw herself dance over the tables, people's heads, and take off without fear, take off over the roofs with her lame foot. But she was alone and Leo, a disciplinarian who had deceived her with his Polish love affair, had no fantasies, and her heart's love fifteen years too young. Her private relationship with Leo was broken, but the commonality of their political work and the family that believed she had married Leo compelled her to continue with the dialogue.

She was probably the only female person whom the bus from the Hotel "Drei Nonnen" brought to the assembly building, and only Leo knew the subject of her report. She stepped up before her audience, including Lenin, Stalin, and well-known Marxist theorists among those present, as a well-groomed, elegant woman in a hat. She explained her divergent understanding of Marxism, which was less dogma than a scientific method of analyzing social circumstances and which relied on the strength of the masses. Even the German worker would begin to defend himself from her exploitation. She saw a period of social warfare without bloodshed, a democratically elected Socialism, and found that Lenin overvalued an armed resistance. She knew the effect her critical statements would have, was convinced of their correctness. As she thought and formulated, so she lived and also in the future would not gloss over anything, cover up anything like her political opponents; she would parry their attacks. The international forum suited her better than the national, the applause seemed to confirm her and drown out the conflicts with Leo and the Party fathers.

No one suspected the woman's considerable fears. Leo had intercepted a letter from her young man. She took it away from him. Leo kept her under surveillance and threatened her. The orchestra at the elegant restaurant had played "Carmen," and she and Leo acted out the roles of a married couple to comply with her brother Nathan's invitation. But, contrary to Leo's intention, she wanted to make the return trip alone, and the beloved youth was to expect her early the next morning at the Zoo station. The first roses would bloom, she would feel like a twenty-year-old and would slip away from her seesaw life.

But she was Rosa L., who, because of her talk in Jena on the subject of a strike by the masses, had to spend two summer months in the Berlin women's prison at 10 Barnimstrasse. Indefatigable, she worked on her introduction to the national economy, wrote to her dear boy Kostja and her friends, adapted her activities again to cell life which, despite her blue dressing gown, she called *living in the privy*. As experienced as she was with cell life, she organized the acceptance of her necessary books, fresh linens, flowers, and mail into the prison. She probably appeared more cheerful than she felt, locked in, prey to the crashing thunder of night storms and her yearning images of another life.

Two months was bearable; then she would take part in the first International Congress of Socialist Women in Stuttgart and live with Kostja's mother. Afterwards meet Lenin again at the International Socialist Congress and in September travel to Essen to the Party Rally of the SPD. In October 1907 she would surprisingly take up a lecturer position at the Party school, soon praised as the best teacher and be under surveillance—as were all teachers—by the secret police. Would make demands on herself unsparingly, time breathing down her neck, and in the future twice again find herself in the women's prison on Barnimstrasse, spending a year and then three months more under arrest. Ahead of her there were approximately seven years of freedom.

Difficult years; and what is free, when the new-born child carries on his ancestry, living space is increasingly populated, and the direction one takes forces one blindly onward. A corridor through the years falls into place until a change in direction is no longer possible.

The intellectual Rosa L. appeared to many people gifted, but she became a Marxist—affected as she was by the minority status of a Polish Jewess—and as a consequence was influenced for a lengthy period of time by Leo Jogiches. If she dallied with other plans for her life, turned to her passion for painting, botany, writing, research, or took part in musical and theater life in the capital with her arts-enthusiast friends without neglecting her duties she bridged a period of time in which what was essential to her—love and revolution—was denied.

Once her fifteen-year smothering little war with Leo had ended, it disgusted her to rub shoulders with him when he demanded the use of their joint library in the green room for days at a time. She was finally able to free herself from his visits in September 1909. *I don't have the strength to endure this back and forth stress any longer.* They exchanged letters, at first merely business-related, without salutation or signature, but years later they held personal information again.

And perhaps the love affair with Kostja was a more passionate departure from her unlived youth, which she carried over to him, wanting to relive it with the young man, an affair that ended with a painful renunciation. To walk hand in hand with him through the distant Masai country remained a beautiful dream. She let the now-aloof Kostja go, wanted to know him only cheerful and happy, assured him that her friendship would last as long as he wished it and as long as she lived.

I don't want to involve my heart so much any more.

She lived, at home or away, so turned in on herself, she wrote to the youth, that when she was out walking she had to remind herself where she was. She concentrated her entire being on her work: the winter semester at the Party school. A book on the history of Poland and one about the national economy. Daily texts and talks. She had arrived at herself.

But the boy needed his fantasizing, strong advisor, her loving care, reports, even if the love moon hardly shone any more. The woman's letters told of flowers, clouds, animals, of trips by car with friends, of her work, and most of all of the well-being of her cat Mimi, who asked with "Cru" about the young man, could read his letters with her nose and sent him her greetings. Mimi in the child's role and little Kostja the addressee to whom her pranks, games, her constipation, her character were reported in detail. Mimi bravely cared for the woman when she lay in bed with a sprained foot and could not get up. She fantasized a quiet life with Mimi while her yearning whirled after the extended working trip to Genoa, imagined new trips: South Africa, central Asia, the Caucasus, away from the small-minded Party leadership, the oppressive German narrowness.

A change of location, distance, too, from the too-near Kautsky family. She gave up her apartment, the red and green rooms heavy with memories, and moved into the country-like Südende. As devoted admirers the pianist and singer Hugo Faisst, the physician Hans Diefenbach, the artist Hans Kautsky, and others. In October 1911 her last journey with the melancholy Kostja to Corsica.

20. Instead of years of love, years of fighting for Rosa L., who attacked the armament politics of Wilhelm II and his colonial hunger in talks and articles, saw the world war coming and hoped for the revolutionary earthquake in Germany. She avoided no exertion, traveled through Germany and understood the enthusiasm during her meetings as the voice of the people, wanted it to become radical, to go into the offensive. Instead of the imperial kingdom the republic. She positioned herself with her strategy against the Party solution and was rebuffed. Only when she was on the road did the solitary woman feel victorious. She wrote articles or caricatured her fellow travelers and earned herself a rousing *Secolo* at the railroad station. Her new black traveling dress, black silk blouse, new gloves, and a little straw hat made her entrance perfect.

A winning, unsparing rebel who pitted herself against her Party leaders, attacked them as hesitant and cowardly, above all her friend of many years Karl Kautsky, who dismissed the notion of a mass strike as mass madness.

What more? she titled her campaign, and Kautsky answered with *What now?* They had become political opponents who fought with pointed pen and did not shy away from intrigue. He rejected the publication of her manuscripts or hesitated over their printing or commented on her text. She quoted from letters that were not intended for publication and would be deadly for K.K. and hoped, as she wrote to Leo Jogiches, that she would defeat him.

Blows, defeat, word fencing that emphasized feeling instead of a professional debate. The leading politicians called her a perverse, ambitious dogmatist and aligned themselves against her. The friendly support of SPD executives was lost. Kautsky had to step down from the political stage for several months because of a nervous collapse, and Luise K. had to cope with the difficult balance between her husband and her friend Rosa.

The solitary woman against the many, with the exception of a few friends. And she firmly decided not to back away from her political point of view. Her heart might rebel, migraines or a depression lay her low, *everything to keep me down*. She would see it through to the end, anesthetize her sick heart, let herself be *totally swallowed up* by the crowds at gatherings, get through the election. And forget her nerves, heart cramps, depressions. In this Party, she thought, one dare not be victorious, they would forgive no one for that.

She was too intelligent, too direct, too extreme, too rebellious, too good a speaker, too convincing. And she was a woman who, at a Party meeting, could wax enthusiastic about a hat in a showroom window and purchase it. A Polish Jewess who fought for an international socialism in the pre-war period, deviated from the German camp. A woman who was observed, criticized, feared; who put up with attacks on her unconventional private life or her ancestry. Who lost influence when pushed to the edge but did not plunge into silence. A strategist who played out her cards effectively in the spotlight of the speakers' platform and in her texts, which finally were unable to find a forum. As a counter measure she and her Polish comrades, Franz Mehring, Julian Marchlewski, Leo Jogiches founded the *Sozialdemocratische Korrespondenz*, which, when copied and distributed in 1913, found favor with many readers.

When she began something she wanted to see the effect, she once mentioned to Leo, and put up with the consequences. For this Socialist sacrifice was part of the job. The feverish climate of the pre-war period was comparable to a minefield. War birds on the balcony. The power struggles of European countries for the colonies. The growing discomfort over the armament competition in the country. And the vigilant Rosa L. out in front. In only four summer months she published her work, *Die Akkumulation des Kapitals*. The rapid updating of material was intoxicating for her, as if someone were guiding her pen. And the mostly uncomprehending critiques following publication scarcely surprised her, she put her hope in a later time when social and economic events confirmed her analysis.

Her male companions continued to hold back despite her warning voice, irritably called her a poisonous bitch; but she was not to be intimidated, remained true to her goals as an honest intellectual. For society to change, the consciousness of the individual must change, revolutionize against the impoverishment that was illustrated for them again and again.

The mass poisoning caused by smoked herring that had spoiled and cheap alcoholic drinks, *workers, workers, nothing but workers* in Berlin's homeless asylum at Christmas 1912 was an example for her of the disparity of classes. Good care and life satisfactions up to the end or scorpions of hunger and death. The actual poisonous bacillus was called capitalistic social order. Her accusation was filled with horror and sympathy for the victims.

Before the new year had entered with the sound of bells, 150 homeless people were in the throes of death, 70 had died.

Who, besides Leo, suspected that behind the mask of this iron fighter she was often exhausted and depressive, her stomach rebelled, and she worried about her cat, Mimi. That she yearned for her botany studies in the field at Südende, for scientific work, for tenderness, for everything that she called life. She cherished all the more her holiday and work periods in the Swiss mountains or in Clarens at Lake Geneva; for Leo it was no longer pertinent; for her it was a lovely memory.

21. The vineyards on the slope still winter bare. But the woman on reconnaissance wore a straw hat for protection from the abundance of light that enticed the salamander to sunbathe and allowed the white-starred narcissus fields to overflow. She crouched before the forget-me-nots and primroses and resembled a glowing young girl introducing a good-looking companion to her old friends, whom she finds again in April 1914, unharmed after a long absence.

Time in the sun since she had arrived in Clarens, rented a room with a balcony that overlooked the lake's filmy surface, where she could see her cloud animals. At first sailboats, fishermens' barges, and passenger ships that churned the calm water. On the opposite shore the slanted line of snow peaks cut into the horizon in postcard perfection. Daily her eyes on the panorama in changing light, the glowing colors of its exit, the eternal play of nature that gave her a different feel for time. Perhaps she let herself forget that she had been sentenced on the twentieth of February to a year in prison.

She had suspected the consequences in September 1912 when in Frankfurt's Bockenheim she cried out the pregnant sentence:

Whenever it is expected of us that we raise our weapons of murder against our French or other brothers, then we will cry: "We won't do it!"

Yet she would not take back a word of her speech, would warn as long as there was still time and people were not being driven like cattle to the slaughter on the battlefield. Her person would thus be made mute on the eve of the First World War. She was too prominent, too international, had the ability to draw too many people to her cause. And hadn't she, a month after her sentencing, denounced in Freiburg the mistreatment of soldiers in the Prussian Army and brought on herself another prison sentence? A fellow citizen without a country, an enemy of the state, dangerously clever and articulate, whose forum had to be removed.

She had stood resolute before the tribunal of the royal district court of Frankfurt, a dainty woman between her defenders, Paul Levi and Kurt Rosenfeld. She heard that, as "Red Rosa," she was counted as the most radical essence of the Social Democrats, that she agitated for mutiny and mass strikes and her anti-militaristic stance was to be sentenced harshly as inimical to the state. Her defenders compared the trial to the time of the Reformation, in which revivalists had been chained to the rack and hanged. Rosa L. called for social and political revolution, wanted the working masses to be enlightened, to make them conscious of class interests and historical development; whoever condemned that was against progress.

When the clear, penetrating voice of the accused grew louder, the tension in the room was reminiscent of a predator's performance in the circus, when the audience cannot know whether the trainer will emerge unscathed. She did not plead for herself or the amount of punishment imposed; when she spoke, it was of the ideal of a socialistic order of society in which war and militarism were made impossible by the decision of the people. A mass strike was a stage in the class conflict, strengthened the workers vis-à-vis their rights, emancipated them. The revolutionary Social Democrats would demand the abolition of the standing army, because war was barbaric and reactionary, and the fighters of the war were always the people, not just the military wearing the king's coat.

The accused, whom one wanted to remove from public life, became the superior victor when her fiery speech was made public in the Party press. She knew that she had handled herself well and hoped that the flame of her talk against the war had made a broad impression. She put up with the fourteen months of prison time, although her attorneys submitted an appeal.

She was soon traveling through Germany to protest gatherings against the Frankfurt judgment, always under the surveillance of her opponents' informers. Her additional punishment from the war minister because of insult to the officers and non-commissioned officer corps was in reference to her Freiburg talk in March, but she looked forward to the trial in June, where militarism again stood in the pillory. Her attorneys would confront the district attorney with over a thousand soldiers who were in the courtroom to testify to mistreatment.

Thirty thousand witnesses were available, besides. Basically the officers of the Prussian Army would sit on the accused's bench as slave-drivers of soldiers and the real accused would emerge as the attorney of the victims.

But for now she was still in Clarens and happy with her attorney, Paul Levi. Since the trial in February they had become intimate, and the sounds of ants building a nest seemed to drown out the current hectic news. It was Spring, and she knew she was loved. The call of the gold thrush, the monotonous trill of the lark, the murmur of the tongues of waves on the lake, all these formed the other world, her trusted world. And the backdrop of mountains, their eternal ice fields on the opposite shore too distant for her to feel cold when she sat on her terrace and perhaps dreamed. Across from her, her lover, twelve years younger, son of a Jewish banker. A cultivated intellectual, as multi-talented as she. A seductive man, much sought after, who could listen and was clever enough to understand how to strategize. He became her advisor and admired her. After their love affair and until his tragic death he would remain her friend. Finally no Babylon between woman and man. Instead of power wranglings an equivalent dialog, even if it was sometimes difficult for the woman on fire not to monopolize it with her thoughts but leave him room to express his.

She could not suspect that this was her last holiday, nothing of the assassination of the Austrian successor to the throne, Archduke Franz Ferdinand and his wife on 28 June 1914, the day before her second trial was to begin. It was delayed for an indeterminate time and finally was discontinued entirely on the 17th of August. But the downward spiral went on. The third complaint spoke of high treason, and the anti-war rallies continued. Twice more she traveled to Brussels and was present at the last session of the International Socialist Bureau in July. Increasingly her powerlessness vis-à-vis contemporary events.

On the first of August the mobilization of the German Army and the Imperial Navy. Emperor Wilhelm II declared war on Russia, and on the third of August on neighboring France just hours after his troops had descended on neutral Belgium. The Social Democrats in the parliament agreed to war credit and renounced wage strikes for the duration of the war. The red paint was peeled off, the Emperor noticed with satisfaction, and the good Germans had come to the fore. Millions followed the call to arms for murder, not only in Germany. Comrades were split into nations. The ideals of internationality stamped out in march formation by the tossing of dice.

The solitary woman thought of the reservists hurrying off with their little suitcases, accompanied by wives and children until late at night. All of them in the mood for departure, in the wake of events that they seemed not to comprehend. Enthusiasm for the Fatherland, the mass self-deception of heroism, and a swift victory. Her years of warning about the war was in vain. The emancipation of the masses an illusion, the strong social democracy split into three camps. Kostja, disillusioned, wanted to leave the Party. She had thought about his departure from the Party, she wrote, and wondered whether the big child perhaps also wanted to leave humankind? In events of this historical dimension the solitary woman carried no weight. However, she pondered her death on the day of the march into Belgium. It should be a turning point. Warning and protest. She had kept this from the small group of her fellow fighters and friends.

The young Hans Diefenbach and Maxim Zetkin had already said their good-byes to her, she received the first letters about the tumult of slaughter and executions. When would Kostja or Paul Levi be drawn in? The city grew emptier every day, it appeared to be inhabited only by children, the very old, and women. But she went on stubbornly living, working; when struck fight back with those of like mind such as Leo Jogiches, Karl Liebknecht, Clara Zetkin, Paul Levi, or Franz Mehring. Continued to publish the *Korrespondenz*, to transmit to foreign Party presses as well as her comrades her standpoint on the folly of war. She would never give up her efforts to communicate across the border, would remain in dialog with people, animals, nature. A telephone had been installed in the house recently. And as usual Mimi swung at the light reflected from the crystal ball. On the little table in front of the mirror a luminous, voluptuous bouquet of evergreens and red geraniums from the fields of Südende in a soup tureen.

Since the beginning of the war the Party school had closed. She had no fixed income but more time, which she wanted to utilize effectively in order to write the *Einführung in die Nationalökonomie* and a work about the war.

A book … that neither man nor woman has read, not even the oldest people, a book that will smash this flock with a crushing blow.

She would struggle through, also without her maid Gertrud Zlottko, whom she had taught to paint landscapes until she gave up housework. Perfectly quiet days with Mimi. The chance to walk, read, do scientific work, had it not been for her constant restlessness, which drove her again to assemblies and sessions. And the knowledge that the appeal of her sentence was rejected; the summons to begin her prison term could reach her any day.

Posen

22. The houses as gray with rain as the sky over Poznan, formerly Posen, functional buildings from the post-war period. In between them the old gables and church towers. Nearby the gigantic obstructing fields of parked cars, a gas station, and a parking garage, the circling metal machines. A city landscape observed from the hotel tower that appeared as interchangeable as the roar and rush of a vehicular stream or the mediocre accommodations of the house that reminded me of a rough youth hostel where comfort was taken for effeminacy. Or was it more a desire for the hotel rooms of convention and trade cities? Instead I thought about my train trip through Poland, the friendly smile of both Polish women in farewell. About the flat horizon, dark forests, the babushkas in the fields, kerchiefs pulled down low on the brow. About the landscape that seemed to me like a narrative about a long space of time in which the voices, the tread of the people resounded, their coming and going preserved for all time.

The Nazis, who in 1935 destroyed the revolution monument and Rosa L.'s grave in Berlin—only the metal handle of her tin coffin remained—thought they were also destroying the legend of this figure of the century. And her effect on succeeding generations. The occupiers of Warsaw, who before their retreat plowed up the Jewish cemeteries until the earth was overgrown with shattered skulls and cracked gravestones, left behind traces of their unconscious hatred, which followed them like a shadow. History can be altered, perverted, and its contemporaries can be made mute, but it is firmly written in time and survives its falsifiers.

Poznan lies, then as now, 300 kilometers east of Berlin. For the young Rosa L., sent there by her Party for the election, Prussian Posen appeared to be at that time partly Asian. It was dominated by clericalism and feudalism, had no culture. In the years 1916 to 1917 as a prisoner in protective custody in Wronke, some 60 kilometers away, she would visit Posen for a dental appointment and treasure the healthy snack in one of its restaurants in the marketplace or the purchase of flowers as a pleasant interruption of her life in the fortress cell.

23. But in 1915 she was still serving out her one-year prison sentence in Cell 219 of the women's prison on Barnimstrasse in Berlin, beginning on the 19ᵗʰ of February. Although she had been granted an extension of her freedom until March for health reasons, she was required to turn herself in prematurely because of anti-war agitation. It felt like a suddenly interrupted telephone conversation to her. The Berlin protective custody people could not have cared less whom they had transported with nine colleagues, while the Russian police in Warsaw would have respected her as a politician. Also, on her committal she had to disrobe twice to her underwear and allow herself to be patted down. The cell held a folding bed of wooden slats. Her stomach must once again become accustomed to prison fare. When she strolled in the hospital courtyard she studied the native flora, which also included weeds, as well as the song of the blackbird and the sparrow, which was more like screeching and indeed suitable to the surroundings.

Her beloved Mimi was entrusted, along with her red velvet armchair, to her secretary, Mathilde Jacob, who operated a typing service. Since 1913 she had become a consistently reliable support and during Rosa L.'s years of imprisonment was the indispensable intermediary between outside and inside.

For Rosa L. a new harsh break in her life plan, but as the character of a woman reveals itself only at the end of love, as she found, she accepted her isolation. Her time from 5:40 in the morning until 9:00 in the evening was fully utilized. Reading, eating, walking, writing, cleaning the cell. And finally after two weeks, acknowledged as a political prisoner, and with a payment of three Marks, permission for self occupation and the use of her work materials.

Pursued by the apparatus of the state, locked up, the hermit drafted the historical development of Europe from earlier decades up to the First World War in the Junius brochure. Wars were made. Germany's later imperialism in East Asia or Morocco distressed the colonial powers in England and France—justly—and provoked again and again the danger of war. The fitting out of the German fleet against the sea power of England. The claim of politicians for a greater Germany that would match the greater Brittania, the new France, the Asia-greedy Russia. A German people as mallet or anvil in the world was alarming to the point of competitive outfitting and caused a boom in large industry, banking, and markets. The brotherhood of weaponry between Germany and Austria, conditioned by their interests, the secret diplomatic exchange between the countries after the assassination in Sarajevo, confirmed the Hapsburgs to press with all their means for a war against Serbia. And brought the fiery brand of war over Europe.

The scene changed fundamentally, the hermit wrote in April 1915 behind the prison walls. The march to Paris in six weeks grew into a world drama, slaughter of the masses became a tiring, monotonous daily business without bringing a solution. Intoxication was a thing of the past. The cannon fodder shipped out and called patriotic at the beginning of the war would rot in Belgium, in the Vosges mountains, Masur, while profits on the fields of death shot up like stalks of corn, thousands of greedy hands stretched out across the ocean to join in raking up the money. Business was thriving in the ruins. Cities became piles of rubble, villages became cemeteries, countries desert wastelands, populations became crowds of beggars, churches horse stalls.

In the midst of this witches' Sabbath a global catastrophe took place, the capitulation of international Social Democracy. The German Socialists, for decades in the forefront and the intellectual brains of international Socialism, had broken down dramatically. Slogans to the effect that the Fatherland, its culture and freedom, was in danger, had aroused the patriotic fever of the masses.

The war a holy cause of the people if it dealt with the existence and freedom of the nation, which it defended with the tools of murder. War, a repetition of barbarity. The bestiality of the activity corresponded to the bestiality of the thought and conviction. The agitating news of the danger of being under Russian rule and of Cossacks who tear infants to pieces or of Belgian women who would cut out the eyes of German wounded soldiers, had, as an intellectual narcotic, created the intoxication that led to killing. A methodical, gigantic act of murder. Imperialism had won in this war and millions of the proletariat of all nationalities fell on the field of disgrace. The World War was a world-altering event. It was foolish self-deception to imagine that one needed only to outlast the war, as the hare waited out the end of the storm under a bush, in order to fall again into the old canter.

Page after page filled with her writing, as she analyzed the phenomenon of war and the crisis of social democracy, drawing conclusions but always emphasizing the emotional background of her work. With help from Leo Jogiches the document would appear in 1916 in Zurich. Her opponents could remove the "red primadonna" from public life but not silence her. She wrote the lead article for *Die Internationale*, and her voice was audible, in a single evening, five-thousand-fold. She wrote to political friends and, with the help of a secret ink along the edge of letters, informed them of her intellectual point of view. By these means she remained on the political stage. And perhaps overheard the tread of the warders, the creaking iron doors, when she was at work. With her status as a politician she no longer had to clean her cell.

The visits from Mathilde Jacob, who provided her with everything she needed, came regularly. Naturally she also brought flowers and took upon herself risky courier service. With the moral and financial help of friends like Karl

Liebknecht and the wealthy Hans Diefenbach, Rosa L. gave the impression of being unconquerable. But she perhaps took it upon herself to appear stronger than she was, when she advised her correspondents to remain fresh and cheerful. Recommended courage and serenity.

I truly fear nothing any more.

Perhaps there were magic spells or formulas with which she penetrated the cell walls and her seclusion. The silent nights where darkness became a burial chamber that enclosed her far from all of life and all of life's signals, robbed her of her own thoughts. But a political leader and revolutionary does not permit herself any sign of weakness. She was well aware of her central function, and in prison she remained the stabilizing element of anti-militarism, its driving force. Hadn't the child Róża already made an excellent job of covering up her lame foot and compensated for it with intellectual superiority? With strength of will and discipline she withstood the period of her seventh incarceration and in February 1916 was set free. But how long would the Prussian Minister of the Interior and the President of the Berlin Police suffer the war opponent to remain free? Weren't her charisma and her writings and speeches a danger to public security, and would they inspire new anti-war demonstrations?

In June her brochure, *Die Krise der Sozialdemocratie*, appeared in Zurich under the pseudonym of Junius and became known throughout Europe. A stern indictment against the barbaric war, imperialism.

The dividends rise and the proletarians fall.

24. Rehn had volunteered for service at the outbreak of war. The late, incomplete notes that he left behind tell me what he saw and heard. Employed at the Hotel Wagner in Munich with its foreign guests primarily from France and America, he took possession of his last pay (in gold) from the hotel porter at the end of July. The assassination in Sarajevo caused an early departure of the guests, and a young Frenchman asked young Rehn, "What do you think, will we probably shoot at each other?" He did not wait for an answer.

In the city anxiety about the war rose, the most eager thought themselves surrounded by spies and practiced personal justice. Tension-riddled people waited outside the newspaper office for the latest news. When the Austrian explanation of war on Serbia became known, wild jubilation soared, and Rehn was part of it. Someone cried out the slogan, "Austrian Embassy," and the crowd formed up. Someone began the "Wacht am Rhein," and the long line arrived at the Austrian Embassy singing, its cheer for the brotherhood of weapons spiritually blind.

Volunteer Rehn reported to the cavalry, dreamed of riding out in the squadron, its songs, the blue and white flag on the horse's harness, his horse, coming through the war with it, and he would take good care of it. But there were more cavalrymen than horses and besides the new large-caliber guns were more powerful. Infantryman Rehn, after the three months of weapons study, combat exercises, long marches, and sharpshooting, would soon experience their power.

Would learn the fear that Rosa L. at that time had already forgotten. At that time, on the fourth of August 1914, she had been horrified, almost broken, she wrote a year later from her cell in the women's prison, since then she had become almost completely calm. The catastrophe had taken on such dimensions that the customary measures of human guilt and human pain would break down.

Rehn experienced the marching orders of the Sixteenth Bavarian Infantry Regiment from Munich in October 1914, as if it were a procession, the men dressed in field march uniform but without the steel helmet. Cheered and given gifts by civilians drunk with victory standing at the edge of the street: chocolate, cigarettes, fruit, cigarette lighters. Their pockets were filled to overflowing, from all the windows of Tietz, the large department store, an increasing number of saleswomen and customers with handkerchiefs waved a farewell to the defenders of the country. For many a conclusive farewell.

Bivouac in the forest. Solemn field religious service, the blessing of the weapons, and the transfer of the regimental flag. Rehn's first encounter with the French on the way to captivity in their blue and red peace uniform, surprised by the war. They seemed to be exotic birds that had lost their orientation. With the crossing of the border into Belgium the enemy country, the railroad stations silent, the patriotic cries died away. Houses destroyed, flameless burns that no one would extinguish. A school in Lille as temporary quarters, instead of school benches the straw bed, night alarm at four o'clock in the morning, and march farther northward.

Rehn reported on comrades and village inhabitants who had fled their homes and carried their chickens together with quantities of feed concealed under mountains of straw, until the crowing of a rooster betrayed them. And the comrades' joyous cries lured the half battalion; a battle began, the killing, plundering, tasty bakery goods. Red wine from basements as booty, accompaniment to the thunder of cannons from the nearby front, which seemed not to worry anyone.

Too young to criticize, drilled into the military mode in three months, trained, allegiance pledged to the Emperor, Rehn moved in the sail of field gray over narrow avenues running in a straight line, avenues of rough cobblestones that Napoleon's warriors had already trod. A lively flow of traffic from the other direction, sanitation cars, empty munitions wagons, ambulances, two-wheeled carts riding high and drawn by horses, which made Rehn think of market day in a provincial city where dealers and customers were in a hurry to wrap up their business. Only the enemy airplanes clearing the way did not fit into the picture, and the large troop of captured English professional soldiers in terra cotta uniforms who tramped beside the avenue through the meadows heavy with rain and avoided the curious glances of the Germans, who moved forward onto the field of slaughter.

Rehn, recipient of orders, in the midst of his comrades, one of countless men in the events, statistically on call. He would rob along with the others, attack, shoot as he was ordered. War lives from the blood-letting of the opponent. To kill is a duty to the Fatherland. Four young Frenchmen in a small foxhole filled with water were the first mute witnesses of the war's daily business. Rehn, who as a hotel servant was accustomed to be up at four in the morning to brush guests' shoes and to beat carpets with his colleagues, had to find his own meadow, was an underling of the Wilhelminian order.

Perhaps Rehn, always eager to learn, read in a newspaper of the sentencing of Rosa Luxemburg because of her outcry, in the event of war to refuse to shoot at brothers, but he did not feel that he was meant. He was no proletarian and not red, actually he was a carefree fantast who took life as it came and would spare a glance for everything beautiful, for nature, painting, literature, and probably hoped for a good star to lead him.

At the evening muster a night attack on the English positions was announced, with the expectation of activating the motionless front again. After Rehn with the others had crossed the German artillery position, buried and camouflaged their big guns, their opponents began to shoot. The menacing howl of grenades over their heads, the impacts, chattering MGs, the first victims, losses, as the war language calls them. But yet, spread out in the line of fire, they moved towards the bit of forest, into the English death trap.

Rehn was fortunate, he was hit in the right upper thigh and was able, creeping, to reach a muddy foxhole where the terror gradually left him. Around him the raging of a huge material slaughter. He heard the impacts, saw the yellow-green fireworks, grenade shrapnel that exploded in the air and fell to earth hissing, a lethal rain. His trench lay in No-Man's-Land, which was later violently shot up by the English. Rehn was forced to change position into an abandoned English trench where more wounded turned up, the severely injured rescued out of the fighting zone by medics and treated according to the severity of their wounds. A gathering of misery. The Bavarian regiment was reduced by half, a later report would mention the Bavarians' missing steel helmets. Their gray caps, similar to those of the English, would have led to confusion among their own troops. In Rehn's boot the blood welled up. He was carried on a stretcher to the field first aid station, later to the main first aid station, where men were treated and died. On a piece of paper hung around the neck of each man the type of injury was noted, and a long hospital train shipped those no longer capable of fighting behind the lines to the rest and recuperation site.

Sometimes Rehn was invited by his aristocratic bed neighbor for a coach ride through the landscape. The tender green of the winter grain matured in the next year and let him forget that he would be fit for the front again once he was patched up like his neighbor, who said to him that he was a Jew, which was irrelevant for Rehn and his comrades. During the drives on quiet field paths childhood was closer to Rehn than the war. Rehn, the nineteenth child of a village blacksmith. His mother blind. At four he was an orphan. Child laborer. His sisters moved to the city, where they worked in a factory to feed their brother. He attended the high school, having lunch daily at a different table. God sure to reward the contributors. His balancing act on the bridge railing of the factory's canal ended in ice water; the fire department had revived the non-swimmer, but his school books had drowned and with them his time as a high school boy.

Back at the western front in the trench war. Of the 250-man-strong company only thirty were left, but even so a barracks drill for the Bavarian king's visit. An old taciturn man with a Marshal's sword and long entourage shuffled past the saluting soldiers without looking at a single face.

Rehn, thanks to his knowledge of the front lines, advanced, found a bastion. Trenches with planks laid for protection from the slimy wetness, secured, feet-deep dugouts. A lookout hole from which to observe the forefield and the movements of the opponents. Barbed wire thicket meant to hold back enemy attacks. The men, busy with shovels, transporting materials, on guard duty or dispensing food, seemed to be pursuing a regular workload in a place where they would survive. As if the human being needs some kind of housing and a social order, his place, at least the illusion, and energy and fantasy would grow in the face of danger.

Rosa L., too, kept as much as possible to her accustomed daily routines during her prison stays. She asked her dear Miss Jacob for Lohse's lily-milk soap and lily of the valley water or a packet of Pfeilring's lanolin, her plant book for botany study, tincture of myrrh, and sugar cubes, her black straw hat and glacé gloves for her appearance in court ... *one more plea: my elixir again! I'm developing into a real drunkard.* She could be delighted by a freshly washed blouse. And chose the material for her new bathrobe, ribbed velvet, dark green or mole gray, which she commissioned from Mathilde Jacob. The continuation of daily affairs and her restless writing seemed to modify the extraordinariness of her situation.

A hundred meters from Rehn's trench the enemy neighbors were also dug in and occupied with nocturnal work on their trench. The hammering of posts on both sides sounded like an absurd dialog between neighbors who have had a falling out and would have protected themselves better from the rats and lice by working together. But the game was a deadly one with rocket flares, skulking sharpshooters, artillery fire, mines that flew in soundlessly, and those under the ground driven deep into the opponents' trench in order to explode man and materials.

And Rehn took it as he found it. What moved him more was the old woman who sat in front of her little house in an abandoned village and knitted as if she were deaf to the noise of war nearby. She took the offering of cake from someone's care package only grudgingly. Days later her house was in ruins, destroyed by French grenades, and she was searching for the remains of her household. Rehn had no presentiment that this scene was a representative image of the century and would repeat itself continually.

Rehn and several comrades were awarded the Iron Cross Second Class, handed to them as a surprise by their commander at the rest area. Then again the shipping out of the field grays. Rehn hoped their goal this time would be the Russian front, but the transport moved westward. In a village church without seats their short sleep. After midnight the alarm. Take position with artillery pack, and general absolution for Christians and non-Christians from the field priest. The march into the drumrolls of three hundred fifty weapons of all calibers, the opponent an English elite corps from the colonies. Rehn felt an iron blow to his hip, he bled heavily and could not move. He spent hours in the hell of the field of slaughter, which was listed in the statistics as a loss of seventy officers and six thousand men.

To be silent now and wait for better times, Rosa L. wrote in February 1915 to Kostja Zetkin, *would be a crime and miserable cowardliness.*

Recovering in the hospital Rehn became an enthusiastic chess player who seemed to forget the war at the chessboard. Isolated from news, he probably knew nothing of the use of poison gas at the front or the demonstrations by women against the war. Rehn was tended by nurses who willingly sacrificed and despite rationing in the country upgraded the hospital fare for the wounded with fruit and chocolate. And so Rehn was dispatched a third time to the front and again the English were his opponents. Day and night their drum-like fire from naval guns, the impact close by, gigantic craters, sometimes within the depths of the trench. Death in the fields of summer.

At Christmas 1915, surprisingly, the cease fire between enemy neighbors. They left their earthen fortresses, came up to each other weaponless, exchanged gifts of the season, and embraced each other like brothers. The simple soldier Rehn and his comrades could not understand why after two days of peace the reciprocal murdering resumed, the command from above forced them back to the fighting.

25. That same month Rosa L. wrote in her cell:

Imperialism, militarism, and wars are not to be eliminated so long as capitalism prevails. The only way to accomplish a successful resistance to them, the only certainty of world peace, is the revolutionary will and the political capability of action by the international proletariat.

The prisoner was released in February 1916. She stood before the prison gate marked by the lightless months. Heart-weary and suffering with stomach pain she limped to the car in which Mathilde Jacob and Karl Liebknecht waited. She was not prepared for the more than a thousand people—the majority of them women—who greeted her. Nor prepared for their cry: "Long live Rosa, long live peace."

The small, weakened woman embodied hope for them. And she was determined to meet their expectations, would ignore the pain signals, in order to be able to work. Without an overseer and locked doors, in her pretty home near Südende Feld, and with her beloved Mimi. Her eyes silently greeted the little streets and budding trees. Her apartment was an island of flowers on this day, a shop of delicacies with home-made baked goods and home-cooked dishes. She was overwhelmed, touched, and, now tired, she sat down on her red sofa.

But she found no rest. It seemed like an omen, an anticipation of the coming months, when some seventy women crowded into her apartment that afternoon. After her long isolation, talking was difficult for her. So many people, faces, they took all her strength, and soon she had to excuse herself.

Of course she was not hypersensitive. She lived according to the *maxim* that if one was by profession a freedom fighter, then prison was an entirely understandable bonus, and going in/coming out was the most sensible of arrangements. But she over-exerted herself.

With my carcass I have more to do than is good for me.

She talked of her desire to fight and work, did not want to disappoint her comrades and gave away the freedom of her last spring and the beginning of summer. If she strolled through the Südende Feld in free minutes, it seemed to her to be *only in passing*.

Breathless days with meetings and discussions that she regarded as good for nothing, as *frog and mouse war of the first order*. The parliamentary party had split into three groups: the right wing, faithful to the Kaiser, which had the majority; the centrists, who wanted to win back their majority; and the little group of left extremists. The Party chairman continued to support the war policy, although the battle on the western front had become a senseless slaughter.

Rosa L. was against the internal strife but thought that history would work for the Spartakists. Again she stood on the speaker's platform and knew she was being watched. There were all too few friends and the like-minded. Her Junius brochure was confiscated in Germany, its author put at risk. On the first of May the forbidden demonstration on Potsdamerplatz, Rosa L. again at the side of Karl Liebknecht. Immediately after his cry, *Down with the war, down with the government*, he was taken into custody, placed under military arrest. The government, comrades with opposing views, and the police strove for a charge of treason before the military court. His imprisonment forced Rosa L. into additional activities. She looked after Sonia Liebknecht, visited her comrade in the military prison. It seemed that her powers would grow with the difficulties and draw her irresistibly into the line of fire.

Three days in June she permitted herself for a visit with Clara Zetkin. She was happy with Kostja, just then on a furlough, enjoyed the large garden and the animals, regretted the death of a favorite dog. She began to count the number of those whom she and Clara had lost through death, making no differentiation between man and animal. On her return trip a stop in Frankfurt, meeting with friends. Paul Levi had become a war casualty. But Mimi, she wrote to Clara, was blissful to see her again.

Back in the political arena and the struggle to acquire a few eggs or bread, her dear Mimi was her only consolation. She knew she was being watched. Accepted it as she did the weather, wrote the Spartacus letters; the shadow figure of Leo Jogiches organized their publication unnoticed. The Member of Parliament with the respected name Karl Liebknecht was sentenced to four years and one month in prison. Rosa L. reacted with an anonymous flyer that the police rightly attributed to her.

At the end of June there was a day-long strike of fifty-five thousand metal workers in Berlin who protested the sentence of Karl Liebknecht. Rosa L. took part. Did she have no foresight, no fear of the consequences of her participation? Didn't she suspect that her supervisors craved the elimination of the most dangerous agitator of the revolutionary wing? Was she drunk with the belief that the little group of Sparakists could cause the masses to revolt, to dissolve the government, to end the war that was already lost? Or did she consciously take upon herself the risk of standing on the firing line? The days seemed to accelerate like wheels, chased each other faster and faster, as if they would roll over each other. Perhaps it was due to concepts like cowardice or courage on masculine thought patterns that had overtaken them. It was July, and she planned several weeks of holiday in the peacefulness of Thuringia or with Clara Zetkin in Stuttgart-Sillenbuch.

26. July 1916 and Rehn at the summer front, seven days and nights the wearying drum fire, the Germans' chained balloons shot down by an airplane, collapsed, still every ten days like clockwork the roll-call for wages. The enemy's knowledge of destroyed positions made the pay-out more difficult. Corporal and bookkeeper lay belly-flat between proliferating grain and tall grass, beside them the box of money. Each payee, when called, crawled over to the two and confirmed receipt of the money with his signature and then crept back. The following night on bivouac in the village a new alarm, a coffee from the field kitchen, and the command into battle.

The English position lay on a rise, their artillery shot over the heads of the attacker into the hinter land until they ran out, became moving targets that quickly approached, that could be shot blindly and that fell in rows, died. Rehn ran like all the others and came so close to an enemy trench that he could recognize the determined faces of its defenders. Without hesitation Rehn threw his hand grenade into the position, prepared to jump and was hit on the right knee.

Someone moved him into a grenade crater, later a medic appeared who was to fetch him at night. Rehn lay and waited for darkness, in his knee the splinters of an exploded hand grenade. He was in extreme pain with a tormenting thirst. At night he moved snail-fashion to the rim of the crater and lay there exhausted, remembered a tunnel that lay between the fronts, crept past the dead comrades and reached it around noon. He thought he was fantasizing when he saw a crate with mineral water at the tunnel entrance. He broke off the tops of bottle after bottle, insatiable. Five days later he was spotted by a German patrol. Rehn was cheerful, reported on a well-furnished dug-out in the depths of the crater, where there was chocolate, fruit, and similar delicacies. His comrades served themselves as Rehn had done, and it seemed to them like a holiday from the war.

How the injured Rehn lived through this time remained his secret; he reported on candlelight in the dug-out, a field bed that he climbed into with difficulty. Talked of eating, drinking, sleeping. Of days when he camped out at the crater's exit. But nothing of his thoughts, feelings.

After eight months in the hospital the knee that had grown stiff was flexible again. The grenade splinters would remain in his knee, sometimes become noisy, remind him of the war. Rehn, grown useless for active duty at the front, was assigned to a Bavarian barrack with war wounded to serve on the home front. He returned from active duty at hay harvest time, fell in for roll call and heard from the sergeant major that four volunteers were needed to accompany a coal train from Passau to Constantinople. Rehn was one of the many who stepped forward, enthused by the adventurous trip through the Balkans, which ought to last several weeks. He fantasized about Vienna and Budapest, of Puszta, Balkan mountains, the Sea of Marmara. And he was lucky, he was sent on the most impressive journey of his life.

27. Monday, the tenth of July 1916. Rosa L., accompanied by two secret policemen who took her into protective custody upon the directive of the military high command, was placed in the police prison on Alexanderplatz. Days later she was transferred to the women's prison in Berlin that she had left only a few months before. Again in a cell, cut off from Mimi, her home and friends. *And I had no time to enjoy the summer.* Her life again subordinated to prison regimen. Censoring of her mail and books. And the uncertainty of when she would be free again this time.

She named it frivolously her latest accident and acted like someone whose freedom of movement, indeed her life, has been restricted because of a mishap. She utilized the *involuntary* leisure for her work on *Antikritik* and planned a series of brochures under the title *Zur Einführung der Nationalökonomie*. There was, as well, the translation from Russian of Vladimir Korolenko's *Die Geschichte meines Zeitgenossen*, and she involved herself in articles, secret letters from her cell regarding the Spartacus Group's fight against the war. Encouraged the fight-weary to resistance. She wrote letters, more than was allowed, and waited impatiently for answers, since the mail to her took longer to arrive than if it were going to New York.

The prisoner Rosa L. pictured herself unbroken, as if she wanted to be a model for her friends, from whom she expected just as much hope and courage. Yet she remained hampered by her "accident" and had to rely on the help of her friends. For shopping, visits, financial support, communicating with a publisher; she had a continual need to delegate, commission, and thank someone.

Every week the one-hour visit of Mathilde Jacob, which made secret contact with Leo Jogiches possible. As the only one of the Spartacus members still at liberty, he led the group. Mathilde Jacob became indispensable to the woman in protective custody. She shopped, transmitted information, always ready to ease the life of the revered Dr. Luxemburg. Because never before had a woman made such a deep impression upon her, the large, luminous eyes, which always seemed to understand, the modesty, and her almost childlike joy in everything beautiful had caused the older woman's heart to beat more strongly.

Once again they sat opposite each other, supervised by Criminal Officer Palm, a suspicious man who as representative of the law made full use of his tyrannical power.

Perhaps he sensed the superiority of the prisoner and her visitor, suspected that their chatter was more important than he could comprehend. But here he had the say-so and promptly declared the hour was over.

Cut off, choked back, the break in the middle of a sentence, the most pressing details no longer communicable, at the mercy of this man, caught but not made mute, when it was a matter of rights and justice. That's what she wanted to teach this hateful man; she was furious and expressed it but finally understood that the man was pursuing a cat-and-mouse game and threw the first thing that came to hand in his direction, perhaps it was a bar of chocolate.

The insult to the official meant a severely restricted prison environment for Rosa L., the transfer back to the police prison on Alexanderplatz. A tiny, lightless cell in which at one time prostitutes picked up by the police had to spend the remainder of the night. For Rosa L. there were many nights and days, more than thirty, that she had to spend without news, dietetic foods, the care of a doctor, or her daily walk. And without a lamp she vegetated more than lived; hungry for reading she stood with a book in her hand in the light from the corridor that fell into her cell.

One year later, still a prisoner, she would write about it to her young friend Diefenbach, mention the nerves that remained damaged, the hair that had turned gray. In the early autumn nights when she was forced to lie on her cot inactive, she recited her Mörike quietly while the city trolley made her cell window clatter, the cell itself seemed to tremble. Unable to sleep for the tormenting noise she listened for human sounds, pleased by the song of a small child who answered a masculine voice.

In her years of captivity had she become a frugal hermit, who could resign herself to a tiny splinter of life? Was she practicing hope? Or did she want to divert her friends from the reality of her life when she recommended stubborn courage and cheerfulness and invoked the beauty of life? Did she feel herself a contemporary soldier and believe in the survival of the Spartacus Group, their political victory in the end, the resistance of the masses? Or had the involuntary leisure made her a poetess who, in the police hole on Alexanderplatz, thought she could distinguish the scent of dark red roses? A writer who captured in lyrical images what moved her, carefully tailored the tone of each letter to suit its recipient, but never gave up her political ideas.

In the meantime the cell on Barnimstrasse had to be made ready by Mathilde Jacob. When she heard from Rosa L. again it was the end of October. A letter from the fortress Wronke, province of Posen, where she reported that she had no money. The cost of the trip with two men accompanying her was to be paid by the prisoner in protective custody. She had to pay 4.20 Marks each day for food. She needed underclothes, books, saccharine, and shoes. It was the continuation of Mathilde's services and the beginning of a strenuous trip to the last of Rosa L.'s prison stations. All her mail, inclusive of books, had to go through the office of the Royal Commander of Berlin, which meant postponements and hampered Rosa L.'s scientific work.

Fortress Wronke, Province of Posen

28. Rigid poplar trees hemmed the street. Forests and acreage hung with fog, the sky like concrete. Lonely railroad overpass, the single-railed track disappeared in the distance. In the red Peugeot the visitors.

Rosa L. hoped for two visits each month, needed voices, faces, letters, sometimes in real pain if she was alone for too long; she would bless every minute that she could spend with friends. Two visiting hours that were to be pre-arranged with the management, possibly not on Sunday, which she felt was the most deadly day for prisoners and lonely people, but the Sunday calm in this strange place was not to be disturbed for her sake.

Arrival in Wronke more than eight decades intervening. Not a Sunday, and the management instructed by the visitors. Day and time long established, accepted by the General of the Polish prison system. A sharp east wind, just as it was then, that penetrated the layers of one's clothing, made the prisoner Rosa L. feel like a person with no skin. Stiff in every limb, like the frozen skies that her warm breath revived, while she had to do without light. She wrote to Mathilde of painful yearning for her cat Mimi, her friends. For being free, as she was in the images she retrieved from memory: the tiny railroad in Swiss Glion, meetings in Südende, champagne merriment in the Schwarzwald. She carried on one-way conversations with her correspondent and shut out reality when she became too oppressed but caught herself soon and cheered up her war-shaken friends.

It is long gone, what I thought to find here, had become history long ago. What drew me to the place of the events? Its authenticity, or did I hope to come closer to the time of Rosa L.? She is mentioned in the chronicle of this prison that was erected for two million Marks by the Prussian authorities near the end of the nineteenth century. At first criminals but later radical leftists and revolutionaries were exiled here. Beside the name of Rosa L. it is noted that she was held a prisoner here in 1917 as a well-known revolutionary and co-founder of the Polish SDKPiL Party as well as the Spartacus Group in 1916. The young blonde Vladka from Krakow would translate it for me.

The fortress at that time was like an island. Off to the side of Wronke, with its three hotels and restaurants, the small railroad station where the prisoners arrived in barred cars. Long ago Wronke was more closely connected to the fortress structures, but the uninviting brick walls with rolls of barbed wire, the deeper red buildings several stories high with little barred windows behind which thirteen hundred prisoners lived, and the roof-covered balconies for the guards remained the dominating feature of the area.

Upon entering the first room we reached the border. Where we wanted to go was a zone that remained locked to the unauthorized. As it was in your time, Róża, a supervisor needed to test the official notice very carefully before the first barred door was unlocked for visitors and, accompanied by creakings, closed behind them again. After the giving over of passes, the inquiries about cell phones, photographic equipment, pocket knives, the opening of purses, we seemed like prisoners ourselves who, in the company of the guard, were led to (brought before?) the director.

For what reason had we come, he would begin; Luxemburg in Pavilion Three was certainly no longer there, and as prominent prisoners went, the Stalin period would be more productive. But that, too, was history, like the occupation of Poland, when eight hundred men here died before their deportation. Long gone the uprisings of workers in Posen who had fought for freedom, work, and bread in the 1950s. But freedom is not everything, for reforms one needs money. In case we would like to report on his prison, he would help us to spend a longer period in a three-meter-square cell.

We were finally on our way, and Vladka's clicking heels sounded oddly foreign. Justice in prison, said Simone Weil, would not remain just for long, because it was mad. Rosa L. spent Christmas 1916 here. The surprising tree of lights from Sonia Liebknecht, the loving package greetings of friends could not ameliorate her long isolation. She had felt as if she were on a chain and during her usual stroll along the wall, back and forth, resembled an animal in a cage. She heard the whistle of the locomotive every day at exactly 3:19 in the afternoon and knew that soon her visitor Mathilde Jacob would be going, but she had to stay, and her heart recoiled with pain. But she soon forced herself back again to a calm demeanor.

As concerns me, I have … become hard as polished steel and from now on will, neither politically nor in my personal affairs, make the slightest concession.

On the director's visiting card the address Róża Luksenburg-Strasse 7. A polite gentleman with a dark walrus mustache who had tea served to us in his study in ornate white cups. He kept his place at his desk close to the plastic telephone, the cell phone in his pocket. Behind him the Polish eagle, framed in wood, which took aim at the built-in closets on the left wall. Soft sounds from a radio while the director reported on his male inmates, all of whom he knew personally. His gray tweed jacket, gray shirt, red and gray patterned necktie suited his commanding voice. After he retired he and his family would leave the fortress area and move far away. For now he was the landlord here and the first prisoner in a fortress city with an elementary school and auditorium, shopping opportunities, library for prisoners and guards, a chapel, and a medical room. Only about half of the prisoners were capable of activity and many had to be psychologically cared for.

Something seemed to disturb Vladka, who had been translating. The tone of her voice became brighter and stronger, which seemed to amuse the director. He answered questions with composure, his dark eyes fixed on the young face. She had spoken out against the re-socialization of the prisoners, she explained to me; she found it too human, too expensive, and in vain. She was for atonement and deprivation, the death penalty. Vladka was a stern worker. She taught in a college, served as translator at fairs and was a mother. However, winter holidays were a luxury for her family. Growing up in socialistic Poland she knew the effort to have a bit of ordinary comfort. After the collapse of the Wall the new conditions were equally enervating; had they made the practicing Catholic woman unmerciful? And her slight fear that she would have to leave her painstakingly furnished apartment if the Jewish owner, who lived in London, were to raise her rent. "Our land, their houses," many a Pole would still say. Would their land always remain a war zone?

At the time of protective-custody prisoners there were 800 persons in Wronke, two wings filled with women. But she was isolated, always alone, a stranger to everyone. A solitary woman in protective custody whose two cells were cleaned by a fellow prisoner, when perhaps a little dialog took place. In the narrow sleeping space her white ruffled curtains that concealed the barred window. Mathilde Jacob faithfully filled her long list of orders:

Please, a blue outfit with blouses, a cotton dress, kimono, warm pink slip, three bed sheets with a broad border, three without a border, three pillowcases (everything with monogram), four wash cloths, bath towels, underwear (no woolen stockings), six napkins (the new ones), six kitchen towels, a bedside mat, foot pillow, shoehorn, the green satin bedspread from the maid's room, the white coverlet with flowers, alarm clock (allowed), brown purse, empty, artist's portfolio (Michelangelo, Turner, Feuerbach), plaid travel rug with strap. My stamp.

Like Robinson she made her island livable. With the addition of her personal things the two barren rooms became characteristic of her person. To remain a human being, to be a human being was her basic motive. In the sleeping cell, formerly a medical room, the bed, an enamel wash basin. Table and chair near the window, certainly always covered with books, art portfolios, notes. On the same wall a shelf on which I imagine a downy powder puff, a little bottle of toilet water, and 911 cologne. Also a gold-rimmed mirror, too small to examine the fit of the blue velveteen dress, and somewhere the closet for her clothes, hats, a veil strewn with black dots, requested of Sonja L. Her books in the other room, probably, stacked in a crate: Homer, Grillparzer, Hebbel, or Lessing among them; Engels, Marx, the Communist Manifesto. A French Bible, a history of materialism, folk tales, plant and animal geography. The variety only suggested and constantly in process of exchange with new readings. On her desk the ticking clock, sealing wax and seal for her voluminous correspondence, writing materials, and her scientific work. Her translation of Korolenko's *Die Geschichte meines Zeitgenossen* and the *Antikritik* reproduced in several copies in Mathilde Jacob's secretarial office. The first copy would go to Franz Mehring, the second to the young Hans Diefenbach, stationed as a military doctor in Posen.

Naturally the reader of the *Antikritik* would have to be knowledgeable about the national economy in general and the works of Marx in particular in order to give the book scientific value, the author wrote to Posen. Thus regarded, her work was really a luxury item that one could print on handmade paper for its half dozen readers.

I suspect her desk was at the window, the table with a cheerful cover in the middle of the room, the sofa at the wall. A few pictures from the Berlin apartment and flowers, for every time of year voluptuous flowery greetings.

At the same time she was a prisoner, locked in daily at six p.m., her freedom restricted to the narrow rooms. And for days or weeks she was not aware of a single voice, became withdrawn because of it, and sometimes thought she would go mad. The way she looked at her surroundings adapted itself to her field of vision. Everything had significance, the little mouse, the butterfly, birds' songs, all of nature. The rumbling of Saturday evening cleaning that forced its way to her from the open window of her prison cell, in between the voice of the orderlies. Poetically specific images as signals of life from the outside. Her impatience soothed with telegrams, the walls made penetrable. And her loneliness stimulated anew by memories, the yearning in her dreamlike saunter through Südende blended with the subdued shriek of the wild geese on the Havel. Repeated to herself and the "you" of her correspondence that her person, her thoughts were not crushed by prison.

The director accompanied the visitors through the several-storied prison wing. Its layout in the form of a cross made it possible for someone at the point of intersection to see in all directions. Every cell occupied, its arched door furnished with number and name. The house master's key opened a narrow cell, its occupants at work. International conventions were observed, but with the lack of means it was not possible to realize them completely. Even the schoolmaster, a friendly giant, seemed perpetually caught between his desk and the filing cabinets.

Perhaps Rosa L. walked down the same corridor we traversed. Long walks in the paved courtyard had taken their toll on her shoes, and she had to show proof of urgency before Mathilde could provide new ones with the official purchase card. Perhaps the old harmonium outside the chapel began to play and brought back memories of the music evenings she had missed for so long, as well as Mörike's verses, word music that she spoke into the silence outside her barred window.

We cut across the courtyard. Only the cats appeared to be free here, young autumn cats, and Vladka relieved that the black one that ran across our path at least had white paws. The rooms of Protective Custody Prisoner Rosa L. told us nothing, and historians are of differing opinions about the authentic place. For me it sufficed to see the wall along which the solitary woman walked for hours, even when rain streamed down or a snowstorm, accompanied by a large titmouse that hopped along from bush to bush. The solitary woman, wrapped in a loden cape, her old hat sopping wet during the rain, which ran down from her hair to her neck. She found it pleasant and conducive to rumination and dreams. Perhaps she forgot the wall and the wire fence that separated the little garden from the prison courtyard. She talked with Hans Diefenbach far off in Posen and wished that his deep boyish bass would read aloud to her from *Wallenstein*, as he had in Südende, *between countless cups of tea*. Hoped he would read Shakespeare or Goethe later, when she was free.

But how long does hope remain active? In February 1917 the Russian Revolution, the Czar overthrown, and many an old friend freed from prison. All the while her glance bounced off the same wall; she watered her flowers at the barred east window; saw the new buds; and Mathilde provided her with a deckchair and a wicker armchair. The revolutionary sunned herself to think among lilacs, silver poplars, chestnut and flowering cherry trees, the first brimstone butterfly. But the sunlight was not able to warm her, and sometimes her notion that she was not a real person but some kind of bird or another animal in an unsuccessful human form. A caged life in which one slowly becomes mute, closer to the language of the birds than of humans, separated from world history, bent meticulously over one's herbarium, regarding a half-dead peacock butterfly as a dramatic event, life and happiness somewhere else, far away. In the evening, at six, *lock-up*, nothing more to expect; behind bars. Yearning in the glance that follows the swallows into the blue distance, slices through the sky with them, dives in. The yearning a spasmodic pain, agonizing, noisy, and constricting, triggered melancholy and migraine before it veered off again into hope.

An early summer mood, as if one were in the Sunday garden, solemn organ music from the prison church in the distance and the solitary woman busy with letter-writing, a ring of light on the sheet of paper and the moving shadow of the pages, colorful reports to the outside world. *Only one thing torments me: that I am alone to enjoy so much beauty.*

About ten in the morning at her desk. Spartacus letters in April on the revolution in Russia, Lenin back from Switzerland, her multi-layered analysis. And yet she would rather *lay all ten fingers on the keys of the world's piano.* Leo Jogiches informed her of all that he would undertake to secure her freedom. A social democratic voice in Parliament to do what he could to release the security confinement of Dr. Rosa Luxemburg, which no longer corresponded to the protective-custody law. Occasionally the trip with guards to the doctor in Posen and the impatiently awaited visits. Despite supervision the constant exchange of secret news.

With the indispensable Mathilde Jacob, secretary, confidante, and caretaker of the beloved little Mimi. Mathilde transmitted greetings from the cell, provided for gifts and books and was her connection to the attorneys and authorities, because additional investigations, legal proceedings, revisions waited. Mathilde was to see to linen summer shoes and a new blue dress made according to exact instructions. The collar of royal blue silk, velvet buttons, the skirt smooth, no pleats, in front by 6 cm and in back 8 cm shorter than the old gray model. Then, with this heat, the prisoner had to have a white cotton dress. The wonderfully embroidered batiste material, her gift to Clara Zetkin, lying around for years, she would need several meters of it, since material was not to be bought. And in addition summer gloves, a black sun shade, half linen, with a wooden handle, to replace the one forgotten in the train, and immediately 25 Marks for the washerwoman. Embrace and kiss for Mathilde and Mimi, a thousand kisses, in huge, in frightful yearning, and hearty greetings to Mathilde's mother and sister Gretchen.

Between Berlin and Wronke lay seven hours on the train. Arrive, find a hotel and wait in the room for visiting hour with all the objects ordered and more. With flowers, things to eat, books, new news that would not pass any censor, waiting in this Wronke that seemed to be dominated by the fortress tower. Humbled, faceless houses for the visitor, who fidgeted restlessly perhaps, filled the empty time with her imaginings. Uncertain how Rosa L. would meet her, whether she—no longer accustomed to human proximity—could bear the yearningly anticipated friend, and whether in the limited time a dialog would ensue. Mathilde would sense how Rosa L. felt. In her cheerful eyes an unredeemable expectation of the other woman. The table between them. If an exchange of roles were possible, Mathilde would take the protective custody imprisonment on herself that was so repugnant to the complex personality of Rosa L. and was an actual torture. She looked after Rosa L.'s needs, cared for her, loved her, although in terms of the time they had it seemed difficult, and she traveled back with more burdens than when she arrived.

Love me—in spite of everything. Your R., the protective-custody prisoner wrote on the first of July 1917 to her dearest Mathilde and wished her a good journey. Certainly for both women a difficult balancing act. One cannot be dependent on people without trying to tyrannize them later, noted Simone Weil, whom people compared with Rosa Luxemburg, and who was envied for a heart that was ready to beat for the entire world.

It was summer and Rosa L. loved the changing moods in her little garden, continued to translate Korolenko and wrote for Spartacus. In July Mathilde Jacob, who wanted to spend her holiday near the fortress. During a visiting hour the state's attorney informed Rosa L. and her visitor that she would be moved into another prison, day and time remained a secret. Immediately Mathilde provided packing cases for books, household items, and the local produce already on hand, and began to pack. She would follow Rosa L. to Breslau, the ninth prison, the day after her involuntary departure from Wronke, bringing the baggage with her.

The prison director had the old architectural plans for the fortress brought out and carefully spread these documents from 1886 before us. They had been discovered when the tower was torn down, long after the imprisonment of Rosa L. Construction had begun in 1889 while the eighteen-year-old from Warsaw emigrated to Zurich, began her studies, and her love for Leo Jogiches revolutionized her life. We bent over the fortress plans. Along with the tower the ship's bell that had sounded the occupants of the fortress to meals and bedtime had also disappeared. Rosa L. never mentioned it. My eyes sought out the medical area on the plan, the island Robinson, the narrow paved path along the wall that she had walked on 22 July 1917 as she left the fortress.

The small railroad station in Wronke lay on a lower level than the street. We looked upon two bands of tracks, east or west. It had been a Sunday when Frau Rosa Luxemburg was transported to a prison in Breslau, this woman with her extremely stirring and incendiary activity in the radical Socialist movement endangering the security of the Reich, who for the past nine months had been in protective custody.

On that day no visitor boarding cards were given out by the railway office, but she stood there, her stately, strong Mathilde. Perhaps an embrace, a few words of farewell were possible, in any case the exchange of glances. Very soon she would appeal to the commander in Breslau for four hours of visiting time; with her organizational talent, her maternal presence, she would alleviate Rosa L.'s shock at the change from provincial Wronke to the bare cells on Breslau's Kletschkaustrasse.

More than eight decades later I followed her path with Vladka in a racing Intercity train.

Breslau, Berlin

29. No comfortable strolls through the grass, no nightingale song, no high-spirited garden cynic who—dramatic as a demagogue—filled her little garden with nonsense, clambered pathetically up the slight hazelnut bush near her barred window, and was called *sweet blabbermouth* by the solitary woman.

Instead of the small-town atmosphere of Wronke the gloomy brick structures, several stories high, sections in a cross or y-form. In the center the lookout guardhouse. Rosa L., the protective-custody prisoner, was allocated two cells as sleeping and work space in Section Y, Pavilion 2, and each one was locked behind her. If she wanted to change cells she had to make it known by knocking, but the supervisor was not always available. Her free space had narrowed. The strolls in the courtyard between prison buildings, with daily business activities going on and women working in prison uniforms precluded any daydreaming, and she thought that she was being treated like a prisoner herself. Her eyes cast down at the gray pavement she made her way listlessly and would soon find herself in time niches where the autumnal early sunset blurred the wings of the prison, the prisoners became shadows, and the moon rose. Her eyes followed the swarm of crows that flew into the fields to their sleep trees with the gentle sound they made by day. And night seemed to conceal the solitary woman, envelop her in veils as she left the courtyard behind the two columns of prisoners dragging heavy kettles with the evening's soup before the lights of the shops were extinguished, the doors of the institution locked and bolted. She reported on two narrow strips of grass that were crushed by prisoners hanging laundry there, discovered grain growing and herbs, and there were butterflies; took pleasure in the doves and sparrows, made herself fit in with her surroundings in little ways. To the northwest of her cell the men's prison. Above the wall the tips of black poplars and mountain ash. Cloud images as fleeting Impressionism in the window square.

Mathilde Jacob provided a clothes cupboard and washing equipment. From Wronke came the pictures, books, basket chair, and rug. She organized food from the neighborhood and the wife of a comrade who cooked for the solitary woman, because her stomach would have rejected the prison fare. Among her constant efforts to alleviate the prisoner's cell life she arranged to satisfy her wishes for books, writing paper, clothing, snap fasteners, glue, or tea, for letters, visits, funds for wooden shoes that one could purchase in Berlin.

You must see that they attach heels to them (naturally made of wood, 4 cm high) because otherwise I will not be able to walk in them.

It seemed that the solitary woman kept a firm hold on a normal life within a small framework, but her trip outside that frame to see the commanding officer, when she wanted to clarify a number of issues, clearly indicated how unaccustomed she was to people. She felt deafened by the traffic and the bustle of activity in the street, regarded the city at the end of August as dusty, hot, its trees already quite withered. By contrast, a scientific treatise on the migration of birds to the south delighted her. The large birds, like cranes, would carry smaller species of birds on their back. Between predators and songbirds a peace ensued for that period of time, which so touched her that she even felt Breslau was a place in which people could live. There were moments in which she seemed to conquer her cell existence with books, letters, work, yet she was uprooted. Cut off from her active life as a politician and from other women. Her capabilities, her temperament as if under a glass bell where her ability to breathe became increasingly difficult. Her great impatience apparently tamed, but unschooled in patience, and again and again the epistolary pleas, admonitions, thankful reactions.

Dearest! Why didn't you send me the 36 x 3 M. that I must pay out here for self-employment for the six weeks in prison? Bring the money with you. Kiss. Yours, R. Enclosed as a greeting to you the "Music of the World." The 30 M has arrived.

Her sentence for insulting the night guard Palme in 1916 had been upheld.

30. Traveling through the wintry country, hazy images. My travel companion Vladka learned English when she was eight years old. Mother had been interested in languages. Later a degree in German Studies, a paper on Ingeborg Bachmann. Her little son could already converse in English. What her husband earned was too little, the state was not family friendly, it was self-evident that she would work. But feminism was no theme for Vladka, and that sculpture of a female Christ in New York was blasphemous. A Polish woman still let herself be helped into her coat and the door opened for her, she valued her "Rosenkavalier." Suddenly the concrete structures, industrial chimneys, a railroad station, hurrying travelers, the sign Wroclaw, according to the timetable fifteen minutes too early. The city an abyss that sucked everything that came near into itself, it mixed everything together like some kind of metropolis that could be German. In Rosa L.'s time it was a German city.

A cold, gray morning. The harsh east wind chased the rain across the pavement and had us blindly fleeing from the car behind the rust-darkened brick walls of the prison that was now protected as a memorial. But the coldness seemed to be mortared into the century-old structure and also covered the visitors, who had to pass a thorough questioning, as they did in the Wronke fortress, before the stocky, stately Directress of the house heartily greeted them, offered tea or coffee and incidentally wanted to know if I could give her the cell number of the former inhabitant Rosa Luxemburg. Her motherly face with its bright questioning eyes, her high cheekbones, seemed ageless. Her thick blonde hair was rigidly held together. Dressed in a pullover, unobtrusive striped jacket and a full gray skirt, she could have stood just as well in front of a classroom or a day nursery. But she was responsible for eight hundred male prisoners. Career criminals, drug and alcohol dependent men who came here from all parts of the country to be re-socialized after considerable waiting periods. The reform, which swallowed a great deal of money, was rejected by most of the affected men, and a large number relapsed; but, she continued, her press spokesperson would accompany us through the house immediately and answer our further questions.

Polite and laden with keys he led Vladka and me through the gray wings in X and Y form. Open, lock up, the metallic clanking was conclusive. Young autumn cats flitted through the corridors of closed doors. The press spokesperson spoke of European Union norms and the efforts of the institution leadership, opened narrow cells, permitted our glance at a paper nude and plentiful food. Sometimes a mini-TV, an aquarium, a plant, but to which of the two men did the nude belong or would play poker for her on a daily basis? Under Stalin 1,400 political prisoners were crammed in here, their toilet a pail, just as it was at the time of the protective-custody prisoner Rosa L. In 1945 a young girl had been beheaded here.

An icy stream of air blew through the corridors. The ground floor was used as a building site since the Oder flooded in the last century. The cells and the prison courtyard had been flooded at that time and they had to transport food in boats. The occupants were transfixed into a rain intoxication, locked in their cells, threatened by swelling brooks of rain that suddenly pushed into their cells, rose and caused blind anxiety. A group of arriving prisoners replaced the image. With bundles or suitcases they seemed to me refugees stranded here by chance who had to accustom themselves to the circumstances. Earlier prisoners because of their meaningless present.

There was no memorial plaque, no place that carried memories of the protective-custody prisoner Rosa L. Her time appeared to have seeped into the old walls. Only the now counted in the institution through which we were shepherded and that distanced us from Rosa L.

She had to survive the longest and possibly the most trying time in prison here. Sixteen costly months of her life, which would menacingly soon and forcibly break off. Become thin-skinned, she felt that Mathilde Jacob kept back from her the death of her cat Mimi, but regarded friends' efforts to spare her pain as an injury and belittling. But no matter, she was continually dependent on services, had to ask Mathilde again in the Fall of 1917 for warmer clothes, snowshoes, a fur collar, coat, and winter hat. In her cell she puzzled over why there was now a difference in the rapport between her and Mathilde, who had not visited her for four months and only sent her absent-minded news.

I would so much like to know how you are emotionally, to have again the constant empathy with you that I had when I was in Wronke.

Again she tried to conquer her resignation with letters. *One must remain proud and show nothing.* Reported on clouds and a silver moon, on doves and a winter garden in her more spacious double cell, from which the separating wall had finally been removed. Listened excitedly to the noises of the Bolshevik Revolution, a sharp observer who in her Spartacus letters and a number of articles condemned the bureaucracy and the rule by terror of Lenin and Trotzki. A revolution that suppressed the freedom of those who think differently and rejected free elections or the freedom of the press and open meetings was without a moral basis for her.

The solitary woman suspected that she could die because of her position, *in a street battle or in the prison*, and felt panic when she thought how short her life was and how much still remained to be learned.

I would like to be able to act coldly and firm, without a lot of words but effectively.

But she was unable to take part in events now, tended her herbarium and buried herself in scientific works of other epochs, fled the present, which only reflected her inability to act and only brought new reports of loss and injuries.

Who can know what the death of her close friend, Hans Diefenbach, triggered in the forty-six year old woman, how much of life she forfeited, of hope for the future with the man who died in October 1917 at the front in France.

It is like a word that fades away in the middle of a sentence, like the sudden breaking off of a chord that I will always hear.

Death had cut off the long tete-á-tetes from prison cells with her masculine pendant, when she felt attractive and admired, and she needed the repetition for survival. She kept the voices alive in her memory, the illusion that Hans Diefenbach was still able to reply to her.

The years of life in a prison cell had alienated the solitary woman from reality. What she absorbed, felt, took on a different weight, as if she observed everything through a magnifying glass, although her correspondence seldom made this apparent. To rage against an entire humanity and to be outraged was, after all, senseless, she wrote reflectively to the *little bird*, Sonja Liebknecht. She well knew that the *reckoning for justice* would never take place, and one would just have to accept everything. The resignation behind those lines was combined with cheerful advice, slogans for friends in freedom, the concentrated maintenance of a life model that was like a too-large hat overshadowing the face of the delicate prisoner.

Christmas again. The third in the *clink*. Mathilde had to bring the kitchen curtains from the Südende household and provide the gifts for her friends. The small Christmas tree was so wretched in comparison to last year's that she didn't know how she was going to be able to attach the eight candles, but anyway, *joyous Christmas!* It was remarkable, but she lived in a constant state of joyful intoxication. Euphoria or hypertension, self-suggestion? Ten o'clock in the evening banished into the wintry darkness, into an enforced silence. The mind, hyper-alert, registered every sound: the rolling wheels of a distant train, the crackling footsteps of the guard on the moist sand, someone clearing her throat. Little life signals in the loneliness of the insomniac.

I lie still there, alone, wrapped in these various black cloths of darkness. Boredom, non-freedom ... and at the same time my heart beats with an incomprehensible, unknown, inner joy.

She smiled at life in the darkness. And she suffered with the Romanian buffalo in the prison courtyard struck brutally by a soldier with the handle of his whip until the heavily laden wagon of sacks and uniforms finally crossed the threshold of the gated entrance.

On a stroll across the prison courtyard she saw the strong animals with flat bent horns, black faces, and dark gentle eyes up close for the first time. War trophies that had been caught on their Rumanian meadows and brought to Breslau by train. Trained to pull burdens and with meager food they would quickly die. She stood with the exhausted animals during the unloading, saw the helpless expression in the buffalo's face whose skin had been torn to shreds by the whip handle's blows, felt tears form for the bloody animal and the powerlessness of both of them and wept silently. In pain and helplessness one with the buffalo, her poor beloved brother, in this weird foreign city, while the victorious pain giver, hands in his pockets and whistling a popular song, crossed the court with long strides.

And the whole splendid war moved on past me.

31. In your weird foreign city with the frightening foreign men, Róża, one hundred buffalo were lost at that time, and later, without any fighting, it became a Nazi fortress. In March 1945 an airstrip for the occupation forces had to be built with forced labor, concentration-camp prisoners and war prisoners, with attacks from the air and artillery fire in the university quarter, and ten thousand died so that finally a single airplane could take off with the commander and zone leader of Silesia on board.

The face of the city, etched by its changing history, destroyed, put back together again. And perhaps many inhabitants of Breslau, who had been driven out of cities like Lemberg, remained foreign, like our well-informed guide, who had at her fingertips all the historical data on the municipal building Ring and on the residents' houses. To Vladka and me she delivered a brief but impressive image of the city, Cathedral- and Sand-Island, their churches, gates, bridges over the lead-colored Oder, and in the process fell back often on her own history, as if she were woven into it, the past stronger than the now. The post cards for sale show images of a city that at the end of the Second World War was almost totally destroyed: the piles of rubble, fire-gutted ruins, stone skeletons.

I've forgotten the name of our guide, Róża, but not the dark eyes in the composed face, the turban-like kerchief that covered her head and reminded me of the time of the "bomb women." Of mothers serving on the home front by working in weapons factories when the war to end all wars began. She seemed a figure from yesteryear as, iron-willed, she defied the east wind, needles of coldness, gusts of rain, in her thin little green checked jacket and sneakers. She allowed us to interrupt her lecture to warm up in an historic café on the Rathausplatz. On its walls an illustrious array of prominent visitors. Her home city of Lemberg had hardly been destroyed, she said, but immediately after the collapse her expulsion, and in the bombed-out Breslau the rats as large as cats. Her eyes hoped for an answer as the waitress served coffee in silver pots and the tasty, still lukewarm pastry melted on the tongue.

This was the wrong time for her and her generation, a victim generation, the loss of life their fate. Time was not inclined to give her peace, did not reimburse her for what she had suffered. Vladka knew of similar situations in her family and had probably inherited her industriousness to fight for a reasonable standard of living, a private happiness, in spite of continual aggravations.

A while longer and it would have been more than a chance meeting among three generations, but our conscientious guide soon stood up and with a strained voice continued her sightseeing program. On the south façade of the Gothic Rathaus a gigantic banner, in orange/mauve the name Salvador Dali. Many young people in the long line of visitors, who did not seem disturbed that they were being filmed by a woman with beet-red hair who looked like Cat. It was Cat, whom I recognized too late, as I had done in Wronke, where she was surrounded by guards as she photographed the fortress, and we rode off in the red Peugeot.

The past seemed to cover my present, perhaps I would have told my companions about that time. About Rehn, who felt the grenade splinters in his right knee, his child by the hand, the light scraping sound when he walked over splinters of glass, the smell of burning, a flameless burn within the ashes; his child was never free from the odor. Of that morning in the desecrated temple, Talmud, cap, and prayer cords still in their places. Secret things that the child did not dare to touch, he would rather have his father curse him, but the father did not want to be angry. The child understood that his father honored him when he showed his son what the mother did not want to see. She preferred to remain in her four walls, unable to influence the drama of the following years, including her own history.

She was not on the side of the Führer, like her husband, would not listen in coming years to the bellowing, calculating voice on the radio. And would not forget that as a young girl she had worked in a Jewish home one winter and had been better treated there than in her brother's home. Would share her bread rations in the bakery with Jewish women and, as a strictly religious Catholic, live her beliefs immune to Nazi slogans.

There was the morning when she woke her child, embraced him weeping, and said that Hitler had also declared war on Russia. His mother's tears were harder to endure than the news of a new war, and the child crept away from his mother's fear into a dark corner. His father had enlisted, served in the German Post Office in the East, in a town on the Sereth with a hard name to pronounce, and the area, designated as general government, belonged to the invaded Poles. On furlough he peeled off his Post Office uniform and taught the Galician puppy to retrieve the *Völkischer Beobachter*, throwing onto the frozen January pond in the city garden to toughen him up. The world of action came into the house with the father, and whenever he spoke of the time to come after the war, of their departure into a country with more space, where they would have their own house with a garden, the mother would be silent. The child and certainly the mother knew nothing of the plan for the step-by-step Germanizing of Eastern Europe, which required the resettling of a million Slavic inhabitants. The child suspected that the garden adventurously far away meant more risk than security and was relieved when his father boarded the train for the East alone. Mother, child, and the puppy remained behind.

An icy day in February in which the mother removed glazed pine cones and the snow drifts pressing on the roof that turned the walls of the attic apartment to a frosty crystal. No premonition that the house would be bombed the following night, when firebrands lit up the morning. The sky over the city would remain dark with smoke, a fiery wind sweeping through the streets into which shadows of figures with bundles hurriedly emerged. The dog gnawed on a piece of wood in the air-raid shelter as the strikes came threateningly closer. The house was hit in the fifth winter of the war. Mother, child, and dog ran upstairs to be met in the stairwell by flames, and the Galician sustained burn wounds.

The family spent the night in a neighbor's house. The new surroundings pleased the child, a room filled with books and leather club chairs brightened by the fire. He huddled in a club chair in his exercise clothes, which concealed his pajamas, and saw how the light from the fire licking at the window shades of the bombed house enlivened the Oriental carpeting. Nothing was saved. And the child imagined that now everything would be better, prettier, larger than before, but not even the dog came through without a scratch.

Again the sharp east wind penetrated through the skin as if we wore no clothing, but gradually it was amusing to resist it. We followed our energetic guide across the curved cast-iron cathedral bridge into the oldest part of the city, listened to the continuing history of liberation, combat, and defeats, destruction and rebuilding. The Domplatz with Catholic church and cathedral like an empty Superdome ready for the next game.

32. The ninth of November 1918. Her first morning of freedom and instead of a cell, the Breslau Domplatz, where people crowding together for a rally hoped to see Rosa L. and cheered her when she spoke to them from a balcony. A pale woman in hat and coat, white at her temples but the old fire in her eyes, her voice impatient, young. A first, spontaneous appearance after the years of enforced silence, without catching her breath from the prison world, into seething, long hoped-for revolutionary events. And no time to reflect on her own health, but the goal of a social ordering of society instead of capitalistic control allegedly coming closer.

The Hohenzollern regime and the Prussian "Junker" class abdicated, the political façade toppled, dissolved by worker-, soldier- and sailor-councils. The Social Democrat Ebert the new Chancellor of the Republic and more obviously guaran-

tor for order and peace. On that same day Karl Liebknecht proclaimed the socialist republic from the balcony of the abandoned Imperial palace. But the majority,
influenced by inflammatory articles, understood by that chaos, civil war, and
Communist terror.

*The Revolution has begun, its accomplishments meager, and the enemy has not
fallen down at our feet*, wrote Rosa L. in *Rote Fahne*. The situation was compre-
hensible as a beginning but untenable as a lasting condition. If the counter revolution did not win the upper hand all along the line, the masses would have to be
on their guard. But there is a collective consciousness, and hadn't Rosa L. in the
same year criticized the immaturity of the proletariat and its socialist party leader,
the *Government's Socialism,* in a Spartacus letter from her prison cell? In spite of
everything she put her faith in the worker and soldier masses, in a proletarian revolution in Germany whose swift development would be compelling. In a German
republic as the goal of a first stage, in the revolutionary surge of interest in the
west, in a future on the international stage.

33. Far from reality but clairvoyant, she had followed from her cell the course of
the mass strike of 400,000 workers in the armaments industry in Berlin, organized by the Spartacus Group. Commented in her Spartacus letters on the peace
of Brest-Litowsk, in which Lenin handed over Russian provinces to German
imperialism in March, yet no end to the world war was in sight.

Despite everything keep good courage and head held high! the solitary woman recommended, apparently unruffled, and reported on daily activities. A ride in a
droshka, what she was reading, hearing a nightingale, wryneck, and blackbird,
whose voices she heard a month and a half earlier this year. Requested two
pounds of hemp seeds from Switzerland for her feathered friends, a white summer hat from Mathilde Jacob that she should have trimmed a little with roses,
and three volumes of Galsworthy. Enclosed a bit of material so that Mathilde
could look around in Berlin for a similar pattern and make a note of the price.
Cancelled the mailing of foodstuffs, since she didn't need them, the butter would
only go rancid, she was well taken care of with good things. Her cells were always
decorated with wild- and cut flowers that she lovingly arranged in the quiet of
early morning. Around summertime Mathilde should send the yellow silk dress
in a box so that she could alternate it with the white when she went out. And
reported proudly on a terry cloth robe that she had taken apart, had had dyed a
cornflower blue, and made it serviceable again as a light dress.

Otherwise to sit, work, read, wait, thin-skinned, nerves bare, suffering from a
long-lasting cold. The doves as visitors to her sick bed. Sleepless, delivered over to

night ghosts, to her blind fear for the friends for whom she could do nothing from behind bars. Sometimes a kind of madness that the day extinguished, sometimes reality. Mathilde's surprising operation, Franz Mehring's illness, Leo Jogiches' capture in March. And like the solitary woman he, too, with the help of Paul Levi, would be released in November from Berlin's Moabit prison. Mathilde Jacob shuttled once again between the prisoners Leo and Rosa, Berlin and Breslau.

Increasingly, prison psychosis in the fourth year of isolation, always the same sight of the men's prison across the wall on the opposite side of the insane asylum. She looked passive, like a dog on a chain. The protest in the Senate against the lengthy security custody of the protective-custody prisoner was rejected in a long document that referred to her lack of improvement and dangerousness; a suggestion for a short furlough was likewise rejected. She accepted it without complaint, saw her old world disappearing, *every day a new slipping away, a new gigantic plunge*, hoped for history, which does not stand still, to take her path. Every day a cell day to cross off the calendar, interrupted sometimes by visits, hour-long walks outside, the usual exchange with Mathilde about practical needs. Her request for gray summer gloves, soap, her Panama hat, every day less life. Yearning for the wheat fields of Südende, which had given way long before to small individual gardens; her growing tension, expectation of becoming free in order to be active finally, to be able to join in political events.

Around autumn no more patience for letters or visits, only the resistanceless waiting.

I planted a green bean in a pot; it has become a bush with enormous beans.

On 23 October Karl Liebknecht was released from Luckau Prison. When would the key turn in her cell door, the solitary woman be able to walk down the long corridor with her suitcase, leave the prison. On the evening of 8 November, when she learned of her release, impatiently awaited the morning, hurried out of doors, hungry for action, she suspected that not much more time remained for her, ten weeks probably. It was exactly 67 days.

Everyone would be subject to blind fate, she wrote that same month to friends whose son had died in the war, what consoled her was only the grim thought that she, too, and perhaps soon, would be transported to the other side—perhaps by a bullet of the counter revolution, whose members lay in waiting everywhere. She no longer permitted herself *to live a little bit*, the hour on her balcony in Südende with Mimi before the war broke out, which she described to Paul Levi, was long past. To *live a little bit*—no longer attainable.

34. Leo Jogiches and Mathilde Jacob wanted to travel to Breslau to fetch Rosa L., but train schedules were irregular, and she was to speak in the Busch Circus arena to the gathering of worker- and soldier councils. But Revolution events made Leo indispensable. Mathilde, too, and the fifteen people who accompanied her in a red-flag-draped truck searching for a suitable car for the trip were compelled to give up.

It was 10 November when the solitary woman took the train overfilled with troops towards Frankfurt/Oder. No one recognized the quiet traveler sitting on her suitcase in the corridor, on her way into revolutionary Berlin after 28 months of cell life.

It was your last trip, Róża, and perhaps your fighting impetus was stronger than your weariness, formulated opening sentences, strategies as if by itself. Perhaps the years of your life with Leo moved past the train window along with the landscape, years of love, of alienation, but your work dialog always continued and the gentle mutual concern. The lines of your life seemed bound by fate. Perhaps your impatient expectation of seeing Leo, your long-intimate life companion, was weakened like you by prison, older and, like you, with an iron will. The Revolution was more important than particular physical signals.

None of her friends knew of her arrival at the Silesian railroad station around ten o'clock in the evening. Rosa L. left her luggage at the station and telephoned. Accompanied by Mathilde she sought out the editorial rooms of the *Rote Fahne* in the Berliner *Lokal-Anzeiger* building later that evening, where she met Leo Jogiches, Karl Liebknecht, Paul Levi, and other members of the Spartacus Group. But no time for chitchat, everything in a state of unrest, revolution and counterrevolution. And still no return to the longed-for apartment. Rosa L. spent the night in the Hotel Excelsior near the Anhalt railroad station, like Karl Liebknecht and the other Spartacus leaders always on the run.

Each day the woman of words worked till midnight in the printing office, frequent exhaustion, fainting spells, but she continued without sparing herself, the pain a signal of life; breathless she continued on her sacrificial path, strengthened and supported by Leo.

It was the end of November around midnight before she walked through her familiar rooms for the first time, marked by the long days of fighting and her editorial work for *Rote Fahne*. And like Karl Liebknecht expelled from all the hotels around the Potsdam and Anhalt railroad station. Of course the solitary woman in her cell had imagined her return differently, not in new danger, threatened by calls for her murder and imprisonment, which made her apartment into a danger zone, compelling her to change her residence constantly. No one knows what she thought, felt, the first night at home, whether she walked through her own home like a visitor, saw a strange face looking out at her from the mirror. And no Mimi to greet her, no bridge from the then into the now, time without compassion.

Perhaps she fell exhausted into a dreamless sleep and had to find her way back slowly when she awoke into the soldierly reality of the revolutionary Rosa L., who foresaw failure in her word battle against the politics of the Socialists on the right, enemies of the Revolution, activated by the Eberts and the Scheidemanns. Yet every day at the *Rote Fahne*, the only Socialist paper in Berlin, commented on revolution as counter revolution, enlightened the masses, or what she understood by that word; strove for intellectual revolutionizing, as if everything was still open. Even a failure would not be able to halt the later victory.

I was, I am, I will be! would sound the revolutionary message in her last Spartacus letter and become her testament. She still compared the movement to ebb and flow, spoke of a splintered November Semi-Revolution instead of a German Revolution and of the long list of local strikes that would move like a fire in flight over the country. Spoke of the power of machine guns, dictatorship of the sword that would be the answer to economic wars, of a general settlement between work and capital. Again and again she pressed the hesitant leaders of the mass of workers and soldiers to act.

Don't speak! Don't eternally advise! Don't negotiate! Act! Courageously, decisively, consistently. Remove the weapons of the counter revolution, give weapons to the masses, occupy the positions of power. Act quickly. The Revolution demands it of you.

She gave herself unstintingly to the daily revolutionary events, which forced her into a nomadic lifestyle, and put up with the smear campaign against the Spartacus Group in newspapers and flyers. The demands for martial law or prison, the increasing anti-Semitism, meant most of all for Rosa L. and Paul Levi. She ignored the mobs on the street and became increasingly a person who, with full knowledge, strode a sacrificial path. Surrounded and protected by only a few friends—Leo Jogiches, Paul Levi, her fellow fighter Karl Liebknecht or Mathilde Jacob, who moved out of Rosa L.'s apartment for personal reasons; as secretary to Leo Jogiches she remained active for Spartacus. Luise Kautsky held back; solidly behind her husband Karl, who fought the Revolution as the government's Social Democrat; she decided, like Mathilde, against her closest friend Rosa and would never see her again.

Racing against time. In December the marching feet of Old Guard troops sworn to the Emperor on the Berlin streets. The government outfitted divisions, officers, jobless workers, "Junker," and adventurers, paramilitary free corps, and nationalists, like Lance Corporal Hitler, who later dismissed the Spartacus Group as November criminals.

At the same time the German worker's readiness for revolutionary combat increased and came to a bloody collision with soldiers. A Spartacus demonstration in Berlin was protected for the first time by workers with weapons.

But the first Imperial conference of worker and soldier councils in mid-December took place without Rosa L. and Karl Liebknecht, whom no one saw covering the conference as observers. The majority of the delegates voted for the politics of the national gathering and relinquished by so doing their political position of power.

The united front of the worker class would have to take its place against Spartacus, the Commissioner of Military Matters, Noske, decided. He would offer himself as a "bloodhound," soon prove his worth.

Rosa L. did not condone bloodshed, bombs, coups, persisted in believing in an ideological battle without terror, in the masses having freedom of decision-making. Feverishly she outlined in *Rote Fahne* the tasks and goals of revolution, wanted to enlighten the rapid radicalizing of the masses with basic articles; but she had no basis for comparison, no revolutionary majority. She did not have the heart for it. Too long separated from the basis of the Revolution in her isolation, she had become alienated, a faithful believer who internalized her Marxist formula over years but seemed tipped out of time.

A figure of history who had lost her post, but in key words like disarmament, expropriation, confiscate, and revolutionary tribunal, her voice, as unyielding as the program blueprint of the Spartacus Group, was heard. The arming of all male proletarians demanded words, thus the civil war. At the end of the Revolution the free elections, the victory of the Socialist proletariat identical to the victory of the Spartacus Group, its political power democratically acquired.

For four and a half years Spartacus, the Marxist counter voice of the country, was forbidden but always audible. In flyers, with the journal *Internationales*, the Junius brochure, and the Spartacus *Correspondenz* it attracted a young, idealistic minority that risked its life in the war with illegal actions behind the front. And which now believed that a new government could be made in a *coup de main* and wanted to boycott the elections for the National Assembly.

The solitary woman tried in vain to placate her radical, rash companions at the Founding Day event. Let elections be an instrument of revolutionary fighting and every individual whom the Communist governing body recommended would undermine the next National Assembly. The history of the Russian Revolution had begun in 1905, the German Revolution was stuck in its disorderly course like an adult in a child's shoes. Again she conjured up a revolutionary war of the masses of workers but did not want to predict the time needed for the process, if only *our life* extended to it.

She seemed not to tire, her sentences developed out of the historical past, unerringly clear and just as pitiless toward her opponents as the years had been toward her and her friends. In the frail weakened person the strength of a giantess as she placed before the Spartacus Group the train of thought and visionary goals that had matured and been written down in her cell years before. Her like-minded companions, convinced but naïve, hated and slandered throughout the country and subjected to smear campaigns by counter revolutionaries, united at the end of the year in an independent party and called themselves KPD. Rosa L. and Leo Jogiches, who voted for the name Socialist Workers' Party, were in the minority.

Again a caesura. Her young comrades seemed to isolate themselves from the mature politician's experiences in favor of their more radical course, but she would not retreat, keep silent, would further enlighten, encourage, write reports of her revolutionary standpoint in *Rote Fahne*, work for the general, if already lost, cause.

The majority of Germans wanted a united left wing. Calm and order instead of revolutionary outbursts. The readiness to compromise on the part of the left USP strengthened the government of Ebert-Scheidemann and the counter-revolution, which restored old power relationships. On the side of the striking and fighting workers there was only the recently founded Communist Party of Germany (KPD), said Rosa L., and criticized the Left (but hesitant) leader and main participants in the mass movement, who would give out slogans like "general strike" and "to arms" but by means of underhanded dealings with the government would spoil everything.

Her *Rote Fahne* articles seemed to be written with her blood. As if she would share her table and bed with the Revolution, there would be no private space, her face behind a strident mask would be concealed, so far away that even her memory of it would be hard to find. Was she dedicated exclusively to the Revolution without private thoughts, dreams, did she hope to balance the years of suffering with political victory? Was there a little splinter of truth in that? At least she seemed drunk with revolution but saw its boundaries just as painfully clearly, saw herself ensnared by the Revolution to push on to the end and agreed with that.

Christmas evening in her apartment with her old friend Paul Levi a hasty affair, the lights extinguished, the quiet of a winter night. Perhaps she had been a child for moments that allowed her to be enchanted by the glimmer of candles, able to hold her breath, forget the drums of time that droned all the louder the next day.

Bloody confrontations between counter revolutionary troops and the people's naval division at the castle, and Marstall produced the demonstration of Berlin workers and soldiers, their occupation of the editorial offices and printing press of *Vorwärts,* an armored car, machine guns, and a large stack of hand grenades as booty.

At the removal of the leftist police chief, Eichhorn, by the government the revolutionary masses reacted on 5 January with a great demonstration through the Siegesallee. As a consequence the unorganized, bloody battles of workers and soldiers against the government troops. New take-over of switching locations like the Wolff telegraph office. *Hold on and use,* wrote Rosa L., and bemoaned the obligations missed by revolutionary authorities in the last three days. On the tenth of January Spartacus called for a strike and armed attack.

The slaughter would go on in Berlin, wrote Rosa L. to Clara Zetkin, many good young men had fallen; she knew that her life and Karl Liebknecht's were in danger in the hate-laden pogrom climate, "the bloody petro-lice and breeders" let out of prison to be shot down. Every day scurrying, in flight from her bounty hunters, every day her new disappearing act. And, isolated from the organized masses, increasingly powerless. The second occupation of *Vorwärts* by the Spartacus Group, workers, and soldiers ended after hard fighting with their capitulation and the bestial murder of their parlementarian, with mistreatments and fatal shots by the victors. The defeat of the rebels on the 12th of January was conclusive, and there was hard work for the gravediggers in Friedrichshain before victims on both sides came to their last rest in the frozen earth.

And in the end one must accept the way history wants to run, Rosa L. wrote near the end of her letter to Clara Zetkin. It was 11 January, and she closed the letter for that day. There was to be no continuation.

35. By chance, as everything always happened with him, soldier Rehn had again been washed up onto the streets of revolutionary Berlin. After being wounded three times on the front lines he accompanied a coal train to the Bosporus. The former captain of horses became an officer's orderly in Constantinople, and Rehn would rhapsodize for the rest of his life about his time in this city, which was likely the happiest time of his life. With better pay than on the front lines he could do exactly what he wanted with his days and nights, read the Turkish *Lloyd* under palm trees, watch ship traffic from the Galata Bridge, dine in the soldiers'quarters, movies after the evening meal, or travel by ship across the

Bosporus, from the Occident to the Orient, to swim in the Sea of Marmara. A carefree year alongside a taciturn, mostly absent captain of horses, and finally the peaceful shift of power in November 1918, when the British and their allies landed in Constantinople.

On this day, too, the captain took breakfast as usual and went to his office in the military mission clad in his dress uniform. Late that morning Rehn left the apartment with his weapon, against the captain's advice, and went to the Galata Bridge to watch the arrival of the victors but was probably the only person among the curious who wore a German uniform. The colossal image of war ships of every type that forged a way into the Bosporus remained with him for the rest of his life.

After a few days the first return transport, which went through Russia. The captain haggled in the bazaar for fur coats for himself and his orderly and solemnly handed Rehn a silver half-moon with the message "For bravery before the enemy," which embarrassed Rehn a little. A quick, unceremonious parting, the Germans and the victors were not welcome as guests in the pubs now.

Hurricane gusts swept the mules from the deck of the freighter. Radio messages from the council of workers and soldiers in Berlin appealed to the seasick soldiers to disobey orders and take over the ship. Rehn regarded himself as a German patriot, he didn't think much of the Red brothers and their revolution, preferred, in icy Odessa, to remember his last November swim in the Sea of Marmara. In Nickolaiev then a heated whiskey debate with a revolutionary sailor who did not understand that a man could be so idiotic as to serve a captain of horses, and the well-organized retreat was no captain's great deed and just as likely to be managed without rank and nobility.

The continuation of the trip in cattle or human railroad cars, according to epaulettes, wood, and food was accomplished with stops. The stop for the white guards, who put little faith in the negotiated, easily broken peace between Germany and Russia, was involuntary and resulted in the weapons of officers and soldiers being taken away. Like everyone else Rehn threw his weapon on the pile, glad that it happened so peacefully. Days later the Reds stopped the train, searched in vain for weapons and instead tore off the shoulder patches of the officers. And finally arrival in Berlin, where Rehn's Orient journey had begun. Worker and soldier councilors rummaged in the entire luggage, and Rehn was afraid these "revolussers" could confiscate his coffee mill and supply of soap and raisins, but they let him move on and did not act at all dangerous, as if there were no Leftists.

Instead of housing in the barracks Rehn was offered the maid's room in the captain's elegant apartment, and the old-age pensioner even prepared a bath for him. Rehn wanted to acquire a military ticket as soon as possible and go home, but he had actually no home, no place to stay except for the barracks in Passau. With his fur over his uniform he rode a streetcar until the conductor called out that everyone had to exit, the war was still on not far away. The passengers soon fled, disappeared into their houses, and Rehn was alone on the street. Not far off the Emperor's city castle. He went up to it, crossed the great square. At the statue a cannon and soldiers who warned him of Spartacus people and revolutionary sailors in the castle who would lay out flat anyone who approached. But not a single shot. The Red brothers, reorganized days before, could acquire neither food nor ammunition and probably would have to capitulate soon. With his binoculars Rehn brought the showplace of destruction closer, blue-capped men squeezed past the window openings, and naturally there were victims on both sides. Rehn turned back and left the city on schedule.

36. Much time has passed. The Domplatz in Breslau was continually the site of new scenes, and the city tour guide peopled the place with other tourists, but behind her dark eyes the horrors of yesterday. Rosa L. would have presented the city to these strangers carefully in an historical succession of images in which the war opponent Rosa L., her long years of protective custody, and her November speech at the Domplatz would not be found. History does not stand still, Rosa L. wrote in the fourth year of the war from her Breslau cell. In retrospect a bloody path, an ashen path, and the dove on the tree of time become stone from waiting.

Oświęcim

37. Rigid poplars again, in the bend of the street they seemed to disguise the bus route. Looking out at closely interwoven fog, the sky in tones of gray, scattered farmhouses. Kerchiefed women working late in the field, in multi-layered clothing, their backs bent against the stern east wind. The legend of the courier comes to mind on passing a convent bastion at the tip of a cliff. Bastion of strength. In *Der Sozialismus und die Kirchen* Rosa L. analyzed the failure of the commune in the early Church as the increasing power- and possession-greed of the clerics, who had for centuries fed off the belief of simple people in the promise of a reward in heaven. Obediently but bored the tourists in the bus turned their head toward the object recommended for viewing. The attraction lay far off the road, and the quiet landscape seemed to be tiring them, but they had to endure the ride up to Point A.

A town between the Oder and the Weichsel River with a changing history. Founded by Germans in the thirteenth century and a German dukedom in the fourteenth century, it went to Poland two hundred years later and during the division of land in 1918 belonged to Austria. The pre-war barracks and horse stalls of the Polish Army in A. became a showplace between June 1940 and 1944 of imnmeasurable human suffering to which no language, no fantasy, no horror can do justice.

The name of the place need not be written down, it echoes through the world, is etched in the memory of the living, under the skin of those born later, has become ashes and wind; heavy as blood it is burned into the history of the twentieth century. A place of criminals, of assembly-line murder according to schedule, the death of murderers devalued, divested of power. Human property delivered in cattle cars from all parts of Europe to the railroad ramp of "A. II—Birkenau," for selection: as exploitable slave goods or into collective death.

Perhaps it was chance that on this trip I found the report of an SS doctor about his work in death camp A. printed in a German magazine with the title, "Erinnerung der Täter."

And then when the gasing was completed the doors were opened; and sometimes they all lay fallen together, sometimes like a pyramid one on top of the other, the children always underneath, trampled. And sometimes they stood like basalt statues.

After the killing the gas chambers were to be emptied, gold teeth removed, women's hair cut off, corpses burned on a pyre and possessions sorted to be transported to Germany.

The Jews were heaped one on top of the other and muttered nonsense to one another. They did not want to burn, but it was a technical problem and was naturally resolved.

At that same time Rehn sat in the train with soldiers from the front lines who traveled east, when one of the men in the night darkness of the compartment began to speak softly of the frightening thing that happened to politicians, gypsies, homos, and most of all to Jews in the region through which the train was just then passing. That they were ordered into large camps and killed. The voice faltered, broke, the silence in the fully occupied compartment weighted as heavy as concrete, making the rolling of the wheels all the louder and evoking the image of the barred train wagons filled with people pressed against one another that rolled into the annihilation camps.

Rehn was not returning from the front lines, like the others. His wounds from the First World War freed him from military service, and he did not have to kill without provocation on command of the Führer up to the Kremlin towers in order to reach the path to prison or retreat. So far as his fellow travelers were concerned Rehn was a stage prop signifying, in his German Post Office East uniform, that in annexed Poland a postal service was maintained. The Iron Cross Second Class, the half-moon order, and the silver mark of the wounded on his uniform belonged to Rehn's past. He, too, was silent as the train wheels rolled, no longer unsuspecting, but still it was hard to grasp that the Germans had begun with merciless caution to eliminate a people.

Rehn wanted to end his postal assignment in Czortkow, which was set up, as it was in Germany, with Polish and Ukrainian specialists, except that it used one counter for Germany, Poland, and the Ukraine. He appreciated the excellent meals of the Polish cook at the Post Office quarters. The evenings drinking vodka with skat- or chess-playing colleagues. The friendly climate between the population and the Germans, who understood their occupiers as freeing them from the Russian yoke. Rehn arrived in Krakow in the summer of 1941 and was outfitted with a uniform and Browning rifle upon direction of the German Post Office and now, after travel by train, tank, and horse cart finally arrived at his new work-station.

Whenever Rehn sat at the desk in his spacious room with a balcony, the splendid Kasach on the wall making him feel good and a little flattered by its beauty, he was satisfied with his life. Could forget that his wife refused to be converted to the Nazi Party, and he had threatened divorce to remove their child from the influence of his mother. From a distance now nothing more seemed pressing this summer, Rehn preferred to drive to the Dnestr, a river with swift tides, and to let them carry him. The opposite shore was Rumanian; of course, an incautious swimmer could be shot, because the border cut through the middle of the river.

But all too soon the climate between the occupiers and the occupied became more frosty, the Ukrainians' hope for their own state with help from the Germans soon evaporated. They were enemies, exploiters who drove away the little farmer's very own cattle and founded collective farms just as the Russians before them had done. Even in the little town of Czortkow an escalation. When the SS man's telephone connection to Germany took too long, it was enough to arrest the telephone operator, this "Polakin," for sabotage. Rehn acted as mediator and got her freed, but even his bathing pleasure in the Dnestr became more risky with the partisan attacks on the Germans. Blow and counter-blow. A high security officer was shot in sight of the guard post as he was leaving his office building. Days later the salvo of weapons at noontime. In the Post Office quarters everyone was just sitting down at the table when not far off six young Ukrainians were executed by a firing squad of the SS. The houses in the surrounding area seemed to be unoccupied. Shutters in front of the windows. In the Post Office quarters the Polish cook took away the full platters. The dead were not recovered from the blood-darkened snow until night.

The "solution to the Jewish question" began unnoticed in Czortkow. People still spoke with unconcern about work camps. More frequently Rehn saw men, women, and children with the star move past the Post Office in smaller and larger groups, guarded by SS men or Ukrainian police, and disappear into the nearby building of the security police. When Rehn, a chronic asthmatic, could not get his breath, he sought out his Jewish doctor and the Jewish apothecary. And Jewish laborers were prominently involved in the reactivating of the Post Office destroyed by the Russians. The Jewish population spoke German but remained reserved toward their occupiers; they knew of Goebbel's and Himmler's inflammatory talks, read *Stürmer* and suspected that an incomprehensible threat had come into their life with the Germans.

Rehn in the town of Czortkow was an eye-witness like many in all parts of the occupied country and would see for himself up to the very end the images of murder, the hunt for Jewish people that went on in shameless public view after

1942. The Jews fled into outlying villages, hid in attics, basements, prepared mole-like pits and escape routes under houses; few escaped.

Early morning and Rehn at the market to buy fruit before beginning his work-day. He noticed women and men stretched out on the ground in a little court-yard separated only by a barred gate from market traffic. Plunged suddenly out of life, avoided by the living, flies on the blood run out of their bodies. Rehn fled the scene and went into the Post Office, relieved to meet his supervisor, wanted to relieve himself of what he had seen; but the news had preceded him. And was continually replaced by horrifying reports; a narrow alleyway had become a death trap for twelve people exposed to the shy glances of hurrying passersby, at the entrance a huge woman clutching her child; she seemed to shield the death alley with her body.

The murdering raged on, it was a plague that no one could evade. Could also not evade the truck of human freight on the highway not far from Czortkow, men with weapons sent into the field to dig a pit, the grave for the shots fired, which reverberated up to Rehn and his companion when they stopped the car after a few kilometers in order to calm themselves with a cigarette. The heap of hill in the field not to be overlooked when they silently passed it on their return.

But as usual the required training of postal officials in national-socialistic ide-ology, which Rehn carried out in alternation with his superior and at which, although he found it unacceptable, he resembled an automaton who spits out his sentences when a button is pressed. At the same time another film is running: A truck filled with people that rolled slowly over the Sereth Bridge, the serious faces of the crowd lining the road, the confusion of voices, of cries, last commnunica-tion, in the following truck the security officer, his hand on the trigger of the machine gun. Still the collegial life in the Post Office quarters seemed unim-paired. That the boss listened to radio broadcasts from England was better over-looked, only the snipers were dangerously bold. A map of Europe hung in Rehn's room; he marked the front lines with metal push pins and saw that the Eastern front was being shoved more rapidly westward. Even a Rehn could no longer believe in a turning point by means of the anticipated miracle weapon, the V-2. The secret paper for the construction of a postage stamp location in Moscow was nonsense, the employees of the Post Office East soon had to follow the endless trek of refugees into Germany. Along with the approaching thunder of cannons came the order, the swift burning of documents happened in the presence of SS guards. Rehn left the region with his colleagues in the last train, he did not yet know that he would soon lose his apartment during a bombing and then become a missing person.

38. An enormous number of tourists at Museum A. in Oświęcim, memorial to the past. The international visitors were carted by bus, steered by guides through the camp gate with the slogan in iron, "Arbeit macht frei." Without the sounds of marching feet and the calling-out of numbers, which was customary for the prisoners, they were shoved through the regular camp, past the death block, grouped gallows, death wall, straw-roofed camps, massed toilets, massed wash-up basins. Past the photo gallery of quiet faces; near the cautious photo smile of a young woman two dates, two months between arrival and death. Perhaps she wore the red sandals that stood out as a drop of color in the massive pile of shoes behind the show window; perhaps the patent leather suitcase belonged to her, home address Berlin, deposited on the pile of ownerless luggage. Perhaps she knew the torn children's clothing, exhibition objects under glass. Soundlessly these objects witnessed the events, the death machinery of the criminals, a system that functioned perversely as planned, denied the victims their value and human rights in order to eradicate them like pests.

Ashen paths, Róża, that cut through the land of your birth and have become paths for pilgrims who tread them by the millions. They lead to the gas chambers and ovens, spread over the scenario of slaughter. The poison gas transports into the annihilation camp put on display with date and names, neat and clean columns in the household book for Death.

Jacques Stroumsa's violin fell silent in A major. Named first violinist in the camp orchestra by a camp police officer, he had to stand on a podium every day and play for the march out and return of the forced laborers. He was protected by his violin so long as he played, and his music-making accompanied the victims of the Shoah on their path to death. He and his entire family were dragged from the ghetto in Saloniki; a few days after their arrival in A. the family members were gassed. His song on their death has long since faded away. But Strousma, who, near the end of the war, survived the death march from A. into Camp Mauthausen, continued to play on his violin, witness to horror, would never leave it. He played for the next generation, to remind them what happened and—burned into history—could live renewed again.

The railroad lines that ended in A.-Birkenau, ran from all directions to this end. You warned with all your powers, Róża, against this catastrophic war, endured protective custody, continued to fight, and suffered your Golgotha. A stripe of blood runs through the trenches of the First World War, over the slaughter fields of Europe, the material slaughter of villages and hills, human slaughter. Men became strategic war material, the person dehumanized into the mass, which suffered a collective fate. For four years the command to kill followed them, better kill than to be killed and be brutalized into criminals. The stripe of blood was laid and was not deserted in the century of wars. The use of mustard gas in 1918, which caused the temporary blindness of a corporal named Hitler, continued in the annihilation camps with Zyklon B. War made the volunteer H. with an Austrian passport a braggart in the regiment, freed the street painter from his role as a drop-out, his failed life as an artist. Drop-out years for the later dictator, who was able to step into the political arena thanks to a lost war and the upheaval of revolution. The beer parlor demagogue who invented a scapegoat with his tirades of hate against the Jewish population. Elected to Imperial Chancellor by a defeated Germany, he led the Third Empire into war and downfall.

The solitary woman in her cell had recognized the danger clearly and spoken out against it. Throughout her life she took the counter position, knew where the patriotism and militarism of the just led, that a war would break the strong Socialist movement in the country and serve to fortify the power of the government. For Emperor Wilhelm there were no more political parties in 1914, only Germans, loyal servants who pulled those intoxicated by a war for the people and the Emperor into murder.

A.-Birkenau: A place preserved against forgetting, Róża, a place of blood, a place of suffering that surpasses the imagination. And yet the images, the horror are held in place, filmed. On the screen in the museum's movie theater with its plush seats the white-coated criminal and the small naked boy with a number on his arm, identifiable as an experimental object with death as a consequence. I closed my eyes but sat there, time was transformed by the documentary images and what happened was now. The audience like accomplices in the grip of silence, the silhouettes of their heads shadowy, nameless witnesses to power and might. It was consoling to think of the solitary woman, to remember the postscript of her letter to Mathilde Jacob written in May 1917 from the fortress Wronke:

One more thing. We have a child of two months here who has no little shirt and diaper. Tell Luise (Kautsky) she is to give you some things to bring when you come here.

Mathilde Jacob was taken to the concentration camp at Theresienstadt in 1942, where the 69-year-old woman was killed. Luise Kautsky, arrested in the summer of 1944 in Holland, died in A.-Birkenau at the age of 80. Both women close friends of Rosa L. And what would have happened to her, the Jewish Marxist, who would probably have brought her to silence for the first time, Lenin, Stalin, Hitler?

I walked along the railroad tracks of A.-Birkenau, walked away, Róża, away from the streets of barracks, the barracks set on tamped-down earth, the triangular sleeping holes with foul-smelling straw. Bombs destroyed the crematoria, the gas chmbers, execution squares, burning pits. Man more gifted at killing than living. And away from the pond of ashes, the quiet pond with human ashes, the paths of ashes, at the back the diagonally-placed building with the watchtower that seemed to repel the trains, built a wall at the end of the journey.

Your old Lulu had arrived here during the Christmas month, Róża, candles on the family tree long extinguished. Your time within the Kautsky's circle a moment transfixed in a photo and your memory, with those gathered around the table silent and nothing to bring them back to life again.

The sky gray above the railroad tracks that I followed, flanked by barbed wire fences and watchtowers as I sought open land. In the distance a farmer with a small cart and horse in the field, the smell of an autumn fire pestered by the icy wind. Curious, I watched a graceful person slowly approaching, balanced on the rise of the railroad tracks. Presumably she had, like me, left the tour through A.-Birkenau. Her eyes focused on the tracks, she noticed me too late and, surprised, lost her balance and fell. Before I could help her she had collected herself, crouched between the rails. She looked briefly in my direction and began to massage her leg, soon stopped to examine her camera, shot aimlessly, set it down, numb with cold, frozen. Her face white as snow, her carrot-colored hair like a clown's cap hastily donned; she attempted a smile.

I had recognized Mary, whom I had named "Cat," immediately, remembered our chance meeting in W, the green liquor, her uncertain love affair, which had driven her from Switzerland to Ireland. She seemed angry to be freezing, and I laid my scarf on her knee. Cat silently wrapped herself in it as if her speech, too, were frosted. Stood up suddenly and walked along the rails to their end. I followed her when she stopped and filmed the warning sign, a black lantern with square milk-glass windows that signaled "straight ahead" to the train engineer. Engrossed in her work she seemed not to notice me, then said to my surprise that her family had long ago discreetly told her she had a Polish grandfather. He disappeared in the war, but now she thought he was a partisan and was sure that he would agree with her.

She climbed into my bus, which waited in front of the camp gate, took a notebook from her leather jacket and began to fill the pages hurriedly, as if there were something important she had to retain and be alone to do it. She didn't let the multilingual voices, the rain drumming on the roof of the bus, keep her from reviving the disappeared grandfather and move him to speech.

The hill country veiled in rain, my feeling that I had nowhere to go, the road would stretch out, lengthen, the bus would always follow the same curves, as imaginary luggage the load of images of the day that everyone took with him, willingly, unwillingly, almost unable to put them down, but would forget. In front of me Cat's carrot crop of hair bent over her notebook, the writer somewhere else. I fleetingly envied her for her grandfather, her partisan story, and would rather have seen Rehn at his side. But nothing to take back, to correct.

The film of the century finished, the collapse of the empire, the world wars, camera trips over fields of slaughter, the scenario of slaughters retained, the disastrous assembling of the NS machinery, the long caravans of those who lost their homes or were driven out of them. For the historian Edward Gibbon in the eighteenth century world history was not much more than notes about crimes and the mishaps of humanity.

When the bus taking its tourist freight to their quarters made its first stop, movement in Cat's seat. She stuck the notebook away, took her camera, and swiftly joined the group leaving the bus. As the bus pulled away it overtook the passenger with the red crop of hair; lively now, she let the scarf flutter; perhaps she waved.

Krakau—Kraków

39. The old city on the Weichsel is unchanged. Perhaps its face knew about Rosa L. The broad market square the same as at that time, the warehouses, illuminated flower stands, horse carriages, coachmen waiting, each horse's back protected from the icy wind with a blanket. The pigeons swarming on sandstone-colored pavement, and as it was then the bright trumpet notes from the tall, helmeted towers of the Maria Himmelfahrt basilika. The sound suddenly broke off while I was walking across the square, as if the last note had stuck; but on the hour it remembers the tower keeper who warned his fellow citizens of the enemy's surprise attack with a composition by Hejual until the fatal Tartar arrow struck him.

The city of many churches and convents, with cathedrals and a royal palace on the Wawelberg, fortunately escaped harm even in the last World War. The Nazi occupiers directed general government affairs from here and planned a total destruction of the city before retreating. Rehn came here in the summer of 1941 with forty colleagues and was sent to the East. But how had Rehn seen the city and its inhabitants? Did he feel like a conquerer without considering that he was actually an uninvited foreigner? Or didn't Rehn think about that and was merely the receiver of orders, trusted the instructions to build a German Post Office East in the foreign land, because an official was the servant of the state.

As I walked by, a fleeting glance into the brightly lit show window of an optician who had thrown his wares one on top of the other, apparently without paying the least attention, as if someone had interrupted him as he laid them out. The sight abruptly thrust me back into the museum at A.-Birkenau, conjured up the countless mountains of eyeglasses behind the showcase glass, the dead eyes of the wearers. An image that frightened me; when would everything be repeated and life be more perishable than eyeglasses.

Again the trumpet signal from the tower or only in my head, perhaps the Tartars at the Florian Gate. In the Dominican church evening Mass, the pious crowding in; individuals knelt on the stones of the cloister despite the cold, paused there in deep prayer like statues. A raw windy evening, the crows already flown southward, populated the green belt around the old city. Circling dark points. And their shrill voices deafening in the high treetops, a thick weaving of voices that enclosed me and the rushing traffic flow. The penetrating horn of an ambulance suppressed the other sounds, for perhaps minutes it was audible as it moved slowly along the street.

At that time, August 1905, crows walked stiff-legged over broad fields of stubble, which perhaps put the thirty-four-year-old traveler on her way from Berlin to Krakau in a melancholy mood. Actually, she wanted to relax a bit at Clara Zetkin's home before she began a new *burdensome work*, although the constant need to eat and take strolls with Clara ran counter to her usual practice; but Leo Jogiches had exaggerated his life as a secret shopkeeper.

After the Bloody Sunday in January 1905 in Petersburg, which triggered the Revolution in the Czarist realm and spread to Russian-annexed Poland, Leo had left for Krakau in order to further the fight against the Czarists from the Austrian part of Poland. He founded a war paper, was critic, creator, strategist, and as always expected her publicizing assistance in the leading German Party sheets and Polish publications. Words as weapons, which he smuggled to Russian Poland; he also frequently went to Warsaw, illegally.

For her it was normal to carry on Leo's front-line work with her enlightening articles. Since they had been together they had had daily exchanges, although mostly in letters. They knew their positions, political goals, were companions in life and battle, had no need to hide anything from each other. But why did he keep her so much in the dark now, how in hell was she to deliver relevant texts when he gave her such meager information about what was happening? Did he want to exclude her from his actual revolutionary life? A difficult year, a decisive year for the fiery woman accustomed to success and her silent, stern revolutionary.

My dear, what is going on, what is wrong with you, why haven't I heard from you for these last several days, and even with two hand-carried messages you don't answer? I have no idea what to do and sit here as if in the woods.

She was restless and in despair. On the 25th of August a large assembly in Hamburg, then in Leipzig, Posen, and so on; Party Day in Jena, threatening many appointments. She had to have a few days to rest, thought of Pszczyna, near Krakau, and that there Leo could also make himself at home, would talk to her about everything. Why didn't he answer? Was he having some sort of unattractive affair? On the 7th of Åugust her third hand-carried message. *I'm leaving for Krakau.*

For ten, twelve days on the outskirts of the city, hearing and seeing everything around her. It was her Poland, her longed-for Revolution, her little Party of the SDKPiL, that arose here, her Polonica, although it might occur to Leo that she was breaking into his territory. He would have to put up with it, was not her master any more, did not direct her movements, ticked her off with his rejections, his withdrawing his love didn't hurt any more. She took for herself what pleased her and would not conceal from Leo her little love affair with the dark, curly-haired younger Witold, who had come from Krakau to Berlin. Leo knew Comrade W., a leading member of the SDKPiL, he valued the texts the comrade wrote for his publications and that also had an effect on Rosa L.

But why did she have to confess, anyway? W. would never take the place of Leo. Why so much truth? Was it the old custom of discussing everything with Leo, or did she want to show Leo, cold-blooded Leo, that she indulged in the joys of life now, would no longer go hungry? Didn't she know that her confession struck the man Leo in his heart, and as her breach of trust emancipated her, he lost influence again. Didn't she know that she withdrew from Leo a part of his life? Although she soon gave him to understand that W. would remain an episode, she had slipped away from him.

He understood what she said, understood nothing. How was he to approve of the fact that he lost her? Her time ran on a different plane from his, the communality was broken. But Leo would not look on idly, he had already survived many difficult situations; he wanted to bring her back to him.

No refreshing days for her. Perhaps a little summering in Jordan Park with Witold, who was actually called Feinstein. And a visit to the crypts of Polish kings or her old alma mater and other *extremely patriotic objects.* But Leo's melancholy was always with her; the hard words that she could not erase, would follow her. Perhaps even to Leonardo da Vinci's "Lady with the Mink." The lady holds the animal carefully in her arms; they seem to trust each other. Her eyes in the sternly beautiful face look into the distance, puzzled; the animal's gaze is patient, and perhaps, too, the dark eyes of the visitor reflectively directed at the charming lady, the noble material of her costume, the calmness of the color, the absence of time.

And the birthday letter to Luise Kautsky was cheerful, spoke of the heart's liaison between friends and her wish for an existence without bugs, for which she would be willing to exchange ten fatherlands. Those ineradicable descendants of the mattress tomb's inhabitants would treat the annoying foreigner so badly that she couldn't sleep at all by the third night and now *nervously dreamed of a new, beautiful dress richly adorned with hairy inserts.* Hairy things *here, there, and everywhere.* She alluded here to a Jewish joke in which a tramp tried with all his persuasive powers to be able to scratch himself undisturbed. She fled her surroundings in stories to correspondents, did not reveal the actual reason for her trip, kept the matters of her heart locked up.

Her epistolary dialog with Leo continued. He could follow her in his imagination to each site of a meeting. As usual she reported on her successes, her exhaustion after long train trips; but despite her weariness she secured articles for Leo and demonstrated a motherly concern for the welfare of her unfortunate partner, whose house of love had been demolished. She had decided against Witold and assured Leo that the most frightening events were a thing of the past. Now she had contentment and energetic work before her, and when she needed it, she would rest and refresh herself.

Dear one, be calm, too, and have courage. I embrace you with all my heart.

At that time one could visit the cabaret "Der grüne Ballon" and puppet shows in the Café Jana Michalika. Today there is still a stylish décor that—like the furniture and fittings—bespeaks the beginning of the twentieth century. I thought of Róża on the green sofa in the café, conversing animatedly with the literary types and artists who were said to congregate here, but the image dissolved. People like puppets, perhaps, on the thread of their time. The stage turns, the actors can disappear, retreat into darkness, and with them their stories, their life, whether unnoticeable or agonizing. It is merely a surmise that anyone could say she was here, for she does not answer. What remains are the gaps in the text that is life, the time that is not in writing, her secret thus not to be fathomed.

The August days of that time flowed away with the Weichsel. The Punch and Judy show at Jana Michalika is gone and gone, too, the obsequious behavior of the homeless. Armed with their heavy plastic sacks they shoved themselves with all their might into the streetcar.

Zámóśc

40. Summer glow over the meadows, fields, the scarecrows dressed like soldiers, the distant horizon marked a deep blue as if a sure hand had moved the pencil to create a border for the seemingly endless expanse. Scattered black-spotted cows in the soft green, storks landing and stalking up to each other as if by appointment, they will probably take off soon for the Equator. My view through the car window changing quickly on the way to southeastern Poland. The single heavily traveled highway freed from narrow country streets, instead of trucks now there are horse-drawn carts and convoys of cars.

We would be entering a poor region, warned Marek, the driver from Krakau, and seemed surprised by the numerous cubes of undamaged dwellings in the landscape that testified to the hard work and modicum of prosperity of their owner. Now and then a questioning glance at the road map, and without stopping we traversed the sun-drenched high land, fields, pine forests, and small villages in the paradisiacal distance. And somewhere the town of Zámóśc, Polish Pienza, settled like a pearl into the landscape, Rosa Luxemburg's birthplace.

"Why Rosa L.?" Marek wanted to know, and I said something about a long rapprochement, increasing curiosity about her unusual life as a woman and politician, about her significance up to now; I had even more explanations, examples, images, and was not satisfied with my answer. It seemed to me that I was traveling toward her life, just as she traveled toward the *right life* that was always concealed, apparently in some attic somewhere. Perhaps only the search, the attempt remained, and what moved me to the present journey was unnamable. I came without a firm sense of the place where she had spent her earliest childhood years, a time that, curiously, she never mentioned.

The voices of the Luksenburgs had dispersed long ago, the two-storied Renaissance structure above the arcade on the market square was taken by other voices, lives. The carousel of time constantly turning, the Now a moment that has already been, added up in the end to a sum of lived and unlived moments.

Outside of Zámóśc a trailer loaded with tree trunks. Like a scene from that time when the wood dealer Eliasz Luksenburg sought out woodcutters in the nearby forests, conducted business with the Polish "Junker," the "Schlachta," and traveled to Warsaw and Germany. His early orientation to the West, which consisted of having attended a German business school, made him cosmopolitan and liberal. He sympathized with the national revolutionary movement and was against Czarism without being politically active. Even an assimilated Jew belonged to a despised race for the Poles, the partisanship of memory allowed for no rapprochement; but at the same time he was alienated from his orthodox Jewish community. A man without roots whom, like figures by Chagall, the winds can carry into nowhere.

The life of the Luksenburgs was necessarily confined to the little family cell and entirely enlivened by Lina Luksenburg. The daughter of a seventeenth-generation rabbi, Hebrew intellectuals as ancestors, she broke with the rigid traditions. She observed the Jewish holidays without rabbi and synagogue. Her passion was classical German and Polish poetry: Schiller, Goethe, Mörike, or Mickiewicz. In the home at Staszikastrasse 37 German, Polish, or Russian was spoken, the Jewish language remained reserved for business affairs, which also took place at home.

Which sound did Róża, the Luksenburgs fifth child, become aware of first, which of the languages that were audible around her cradle became her mother tongue? Was it the Polish or was the child already moved by several speech worlds? At the age of five the girl would be able to write and read, but then the spacious parental home in Ząmóśc would only live in memories, the images conveying unfulfillable yearning. For her playmates, perhaps, or the light above rooftops, the familiar arcades, the southern charm of the houses, the lively squares, fountains, markets, the sounds coming from the nearby convent church, so different from the sounds of the Russian Orthodox church and the Armenian church; bells ringing in the Rathaus tower, a trumpeter playing there at noontime. The melodic strokes of time were like the daily life of the little girl's family, without threat. The fortress of the little city had already withstood the Swedish flood.

It was an orderly, circumscribed world into which Rosa L. was born on the fifth of March 1871. The last Polish resistance against the Czar was eight years in the past and was put down with the expropriation of a thousand noblemen, four hundred executions and countless banishments.

Far off, too, in the city of Paris the national guard's resistance to government troops in March 1871, from which the Paris Commune came into being, a city parliament that waived all rent and bill debts, advocated worker protection and free school instruction, and, described by Karl Marx as "an attempt at a socialistic revolution," failed after two months. The hard fighting between the commune with the Pole Jaroslav Dabrowski as its military commandant, and the government troops penetrating its boundaries ended in a bloody week. The burning Tuilleries lit up a scenario of horror that was followed by a year of unremitting legal prosecutions.

Around the little girl's cradle the loving faces of her family: Father Eliasz with his long graying beard, often worried about business matters; Mother Lina's clear, expressive face; the sister and three brothers. An autonomous world, reliable and secure, in which she would be protected when she took her first steps. A good place in which to grow into life, in the culturally open climate of the house, with parents who complied with the prevailing rules without giving up their own way of thinking.

At that time the future of the lively child still seemed to be an open book, being born into a Jewish family in that locale and time frame was not a fateful determinant. Around her child's world the voices of the wind in the broad land-scape, the confusion of sounds of salesmen and farmers on market days, selling animals and wares under the arcades; the colorful image of Russian garrison sol-diers strolling around the large square market place. Four high windows opened the spacious house to the great market; on the opposite end the Rathaus, the two large-scale free-standing staircases, and the clock tower of stone cubes rising up over it all.

An as-yet unformed child's face watched over its surroundings through the wrought iron tendrils of the bars on the balcony and listened to her first tales and verses read by her mother. A sinewy little girl who played with her siblings in the courtyard of the house, perhaps cautiously placed on a rocking horse, slowly moving backward and forward, her eyes shut and—with the wind in her dark, silky hair—she thought she was flying.

The city of Paris far away, the attempt of a Socialist revolution and the swift, bloody end of the Paris Commune that resembled the swift, bloody end of Spart-acus, the malicious murder of its leaders, Rosa Luxemburg and Karl Liebknecht. The no-longer-fully-formed face of the forty-eight-year-old woman, which after five months in a watery grave would finally come to shore, shoved itself over my photocopy of a still unformed child's face.

Is it a chance event or something more when events, like the rings on a tree trunk, repeat, return, come to life in history?

A summery morning in the eight-cornered Rathaus tower, a flattering breeze muted by the flood of light that poured over the roofs and towers of the arcade area, a broad flagstone-laid square, and made the splendid renovated or rough stone house facades, drunken chimneys, and bulging asphalt paths gleam. The city within the walls of the fortress, six hundred meters long and four hundred wide, as sketched on the drawing-board and observed from the collar of the tower, seemed like a model and easily accessible, behind it in the distant horizon the summer-colored country, the mass of forest land.

Maria, the wheat-blond historian in Ząmóśc, and her dark-haired sister Dana, who patiently translated, were from Lublin. Enchanted by the sight made possible by her tower key, Maria gazed at the various constructions with a delightful air of concentration while at the same time paging through the history of the city, which began at the end of the sixteenth century, founded by the tycoon Jan Zamoyski. An Italian architect, commissioned to build the palace, had sketched the center of the city, which was to be a model of Renaissance planning. Although it defended itself from the Swedes and Cossacks and from Germanizing influences, its face had changed.

In Maria's narrative the faces of the houses and their inhabitants changed, too. In the beginning it was an international business and cultural metropolis through which goods traveled from Persia to Portugal and which attracted merchants and workers from the west and east. The Grand Chancellor, Jan Zamoyski, proffered the privilege of settling down there to anyone who had the means to build a two-story house, including even Sephardic Jews, mostly doctors and pharmacists. But the native inhabitants did not feel economically threatened by these newcomers from Europe and the Ottoman Empire. Religious tolerance, made a rule by the tycoon, allowed for the different cultures and religions of the population. Nothing remains today of the Armenian church in the Armenian quarter but a memorial tablet at the entrance to the hotel. But it was, along with a rabbi's home and synagogue, five convents, and a Russian Orthodox church, one of the stone witnesses to the peaceful life of the residents.

After the Swedish attack in the seventeenth century refugees came into the city. There were epidemics and fires. The economic structure and the inhabitants changed. The Sephardic Jews fled, replaced by the uneducated Ashkenasi Jews, who competed now with the Christian citizens for their livelihood until they were excluded from the guilds and cut out of any rights of dwelling and possession. After the third division of Poland Ząmóśc fell to the Czars. The Zamoyski Academy was closed, Rathaus and Franciscan church were used as barracks. The Renaissance and Baroque ornamentation of many houses in the Great Market were lost with the changes of function in the nineteenth century, but the city remained a cultural center; one third of its inhabitants were Jewish.

We circled the tower slowly, in conversation with the houses and their history. The palace and the Zamoyski Academy were in the western sector, which the city's founder wanted to separate from the eastern sector. It was to be thought of as the head of the city, with the Rathaus and market square in the mid section of the city's body, and the sector of business houses and dwellings attached. Partly renovated Armenian houses a saffron red, lime green, or sienna, their curlicued gables, filigreed little towers, and animal reliefs a backdrop of yesteryear that breathes and lives.

Maria called our attention to the pigeons that perched only on the east side of the Rathaus façade, and I thought of the little girl in the house at Staszicastrasse 37, wondered whether she already understood the word pigeon in Polish and Russian. And of the pigeons that fluttered later onto the bed of the sick prisoner on Kletschkaustrasse in Breslau, perhaps recalled for moments the sunken world of her first years of childhood.

The sedately beautiful house, the grass-covered courtyard, the first children's games, the protected exits above the great market, at that time with trees and wooden cubby holes of shops squeezed between the arcades, and the quiet presence of poor shopkeepers. The mixture of languages and races of the seven thousand inhabitants, word paintings for the child who absorbed the images and sound colorations forever: the brick-red city walls and bastions, the gentle splatter of the fountains, the grazing cows on the outskirts. Perhaps on a drive with her father or the entire family she marveled wide-eyed at the friendly landscape as they moved past straw-covered houses with wells for drinking water, fluttering geese, Jewish sauna huts at the pond, a millwheel constantly dripping, turning.

A short happy childhood in this Zamość, enveloped in the love of her parents and siblings, with a theater-enthusiast father who supported Polish traveling troupes and fought for a better Polish school system; the verbal treasury of the great poets, transmitted by her gentle mother who, conscious of her Jewish ancestors, followed religious traditions. Important first years, the future open, its direction supposedly free of choice according to her talents and inclinations. The little girl still lived in a fulfilled present.

The first crucial event came when the Luksenburgs moved to Warsaw, the capital, with 310,000 inhabitants. Her spacious birthplace was exchanged in 1873 for a three-room apartment in a large tenement, its windows facing Zlotastrasse and the noisy courtyard of the people living behind her. A Polish apartment sector that for a short time also stood open to Jewish inhabitants and, satisfactorily far away from the poor quarter of the orthodox Jews, had been carefully selected.

Perhaps it was economic pressures or the increasing anti-Semitism in Zamość or the better education of children in the metropolis or something of all of this. For the little girl the change was a breach, her secure child's world lost forever and to become a yearning. Rebellion against the apparently inevitable, the enforced rules of narrowness and cramped conditions.

A story forced its way in between, Róża, in which a three-year-old child opened the heavy door of the office and apartment building just large enough to let herself out, as usual, with a stuffed lion as her companion, to make a reconnaissance of the village. When she returned everything familiar had vanished, people and furniture, all the rooms of the apartment empty, only the cooking hearth was in its accustomed place. Bereft the child crouched on the floor and leaned her head on the lukewarm tiles of the hearth. Soon, heavy of heart, she was under a roof in a city apartment, where she spoke with her lost friends, whom she fetched in her imagination.

Perhaps the little girl felt the change from familiar Ząmóśc into the metropolis as equally constricting. Instead of a house with large rooms three rooms for her parents and four siblings, the view from the tall tenement limited. Nearby the elegant Marszalkowskastrasse as a window into the alien world of luxury; instead of a small town idyll the restless pulse of a capital. The oceanic breadth of the landscape exchanged for the encircled spaces of the Saxony Gardens, the country hikings with people strolling in stiff going-out clothes. Her playground had become smaller in the metropolis, a first practical lesson in external boundaries that did not weaken her temperament, her curiosity about life.

The family had remained the child Róża's central creative environment. Hungry for knowledge and with the help of her mother she taught herself reading and writing and decided to transmit what she had acquired to their servant. Reason and fantasy seemed to equalize the external constriction, but again in her fifth year a life-altering break had to be accepted. It compelled the lively child to spend a year in bed. Her hips in a cast made her a prisoner of her body, although it was only a distortion. The presumed hip injury or tuberculosis of the bone was a bad diagnosis and its consequences were hard for the little Róża.

The house at Staszicastrasse 37 looked unfriendly to the female visitors, the window shutters and the darkened oval-shaped door were locked, as if its inhabitants were on a long journey. Today it is said to house an exclusive shoe shop for Italian creations.

A tablet placed in 1979 on Rosa L.'s birthplace memorializes the *significant fighter in the workers' movement*. It didn't affect me as Dana translated it, it was as if Róża had disappeared behind the bronze letters, was no longer accessible. Slowly we approached the back of the house, to one side a wrought iron gate into the courtyard. The sight of the stern façade, its windows dazzling mirrors of light that obviated scrutiny. Potted plants in the courtyard had run over into the islands of gardens down the row of houses, bespeaking a southern exposure. The door to the house was unlocked, an old house. In its thick walls the history of its inhabitants stored for over a century, the history of the Luksenburgs among them; but it would be nothing for the female visitors to chat about. Maria cautiously opened a door on the first floor, as if she would suppose a little girl was behind it whom she didn't want to frighten. The three women clad in their slips having coffee at the kitchen table seemed not to question our intrusion. The key word was Rosa Luksenburg. They explained to Maria very willingly that only the thick walls were original to the house. I took in none of what they were saying, neglected to look out of one of the windows, my memory of the visit is a blank.

Leafing through the pages of photographs in the city archive made a black and white film about the Zamósc of your first years, Róża, moving forward and then back. On the façade of the neighbor's house at Staszicastrasse 39, the plaster is cracking. The mere position of the house a geography of aging, lightly, beautifully, like an old face. Two men wearing hats in continual conversation, their hands buried in their coats, a young man with a cap shows them his back. Hands in pants pocket, legs planted wide apart, his shaded face turned to the camera. Backdrop the three-story corner house at the great market, its decorative wrought iron balcony holding plants. The Luksenburg house diagonally opposite does not get into the picture, but the street and sidewalk, badly paved, aligned with the St. Thomas church tower.

It could be a late morning in September, a fresh wind presaging winter streaming over the wide square, a little girl with a large doll in her arms and somewhat shaky on her legs could just then come into view, enliven the static image. But the film turns, the document of only a moment in old Zamósc, belonging to the kingdom of Poland, under Russian authority. The people in the picture perhaps still a memory, a weathered name on a stone. The film continues to run, other lives emerge, disappear, endless, countless, subjugated to the fate of their time.

On the façade of the restored Armenian house the Archangel Gabriel in his armor fights with the dragon; the angel of history, on the other hand, is, according to Walter Benjamin, only a witness to destruction and downfalls. Imaginable as a messenger in the land of ruins, without tears and with a dark hand he extinguishes the names of the cities and the people, takes catastrophies as a given.

After World War I Poland was independent, a country without an occupation force until the invasion of Hitler's *Wehrmacht* on the first of September 1939. On the eighth of September the first bombs fell on the birthplace of Rosa L., opponent of war, Maria reported. She had brought coffee into her large workroom and cut slices of the apple cake she had baked. On her heavy desk a stack of files; subsidies for construction considered worthwhile are given out here. A quiet room, its old breath seemed to me like a long lost friend whom I recognized again, someone who had remained dear to me. From its high windows a broad view over the square to the Rathaus, the pigeons again stubbornly one-sided on the eastern half, turned to what was earlier the Jewish quarter. But there was no longer a rabbi living in the rabbi's house; in the vaulted synagogue, a structure of the late Renaissance, the municipal library. The flaking old pink of the façade, the decorative abutments, chimney and ornaments like an Oriental fairy tale turned to stone, burdened by a ban that interrupted the narrative thread, had driven people out of its history and waited in vain for redemption.

The people driven away, herded into annihilation camps or to the rotunda, the old powder house of their city, where the weapon salvos of the SS-lackeys struck them down. Zamość, chosen by Heinrich Himmler as the center of his forced Germanizing and renamed Himmler City, came out of the war almost unscathed. Not its people. A geography of death as definitive of organized genocide came into being around the city, which Reich's Commissar Himmler visited twice. He thought he might reside there later, as Reich's Minister Karl Frank had done in the equally beautiful Kraków. Their end, too, is history. Himmler hanged himself after he was identified in 1945. Chief War Criminal Frank was sentenced to death by hanging in Nuremberg. Atonement cannot extinguish what happened, the suffering of the victims, their brutal death, and their loneliness indivisible, incomprehensible in any language to those born later.

Bent low over his cane he shoved himself forward with effort, his old, short body twisted into grotesque contours because of the enormity of his crippled condition. I looked away, across the street to the old powder house. I did not want to be a witness to the torments that no one could relieve.

But he belonged to Zamość like Grand Chancellor Jan Zamoski and his black marble resting place in the chapel of the convent church. I ought to look at the man, Maria said, he was one of the countless Jewish children who were dragged away in the Second World War and enslaved. After he became ill they threw him out of a window, no longer useful, disposed of. He didn't know his name, nothing about his background. Someone had noted on his Social Security card simply Pekosinski. Pekosinski is translated as "The Nameless One," and so he was called from then on. Everyone knew Pekosinski, who had been the chess master of Poland. His spirit was not to be broken like his body, a silent accuser of the beast, man.

Above the rooftops dark balls of clouds, bits of paper sailed like butterflies in the wind, the growling of thunder, time an unknown quantity, always in a new mask, veils, and yet unchanged, the same earlier or now, the same bit of time.

Sunset and heavy grayish mauve storm clouds spreading an eerie, secretive shadow over the whole landscape.

Kostja, the beloved youth, received many of the incomparable cloud poems from Rosa L that I quoted to Dana and Maria. I imagined that she would appear between the arcades, like Jan Zamoyski, descendant of the city founder in the sixteenth generation, who met us by chance: the small, impressive woman beside the tall thin man, the female revolutionary with gray hair and the elderly nobleman propped on his walking stick. Both victims of political tyranny, both imprisoned for years, both unbroken, related perhaps in spirit yet opponents. But they would not talk about that, or that Zamoyski was expropriated in the People's Republic of Poland or that his wife lay buried in Warsaw, denied a last resting place in the crypt of the Zamoyskis. Zamoyski then moved to Warsaw in order to remain near her in death. Perhaps their eyes had met, the velvety dark eyes of the woman and the very blue ones of the man, recognized each other and then turned away.

The change of location from the bucolic but deeply historical Zamość to the capital of Warsaw could not extinguish the first impressions that the child Róża, consciously or unconsciously, acquired in a short span of time and that reverberated in her. Perhaps it was one of the places to which she fled in her mind while her body, compelled to remain still for a year, slowly became deformed. Later efforts to correct the shorter leg with stretching bands and baths were unavailing. The lively child had to accept the hindrance that forced her to limp as her spirit became all the more active. As soon as she conquered reading she began to write letters to her family, to the servant; she composed her own texts, which were published. She translated or sketched, was adept at hand crafts, burst open the limitations imposed on her and would remain a rebel and lonely seeker.

Was your childhood a preview, Róża, the first practical exercises for the stern life of a revolutionary who hoped to conquer with word weapons? What had happened to the girl—her limp, her low social status, the Jewish Pogrom, the early rejection of oppression and injustice, seemed pre-programmed, like the danger of ending life in a citadel, in early Warsaw or some other time.

Your life ran before my eyes, Róża, in a kaleidoscopic fashion, the life of an intellectual, of a politician, of a lover. The life of the enemy, of the hated, the misunderstood, and that of the hunted. You were singular and courageous, created for the path to Calvary.

The grass sated with summer, back from Ząmóśc to Warsaw. Incomprehensibly distant that January night in Berlin, incomprehensibly near. In a forested area the waiting automobile, all the doors open, a flat tire, auto accident? The young gypsy, a small child in her arms, tried to stop Marek, who deftly detoured, accelerated.

Index of Names

Bebel, Ferdinand August (1840-1913). Turner, Social Democrat, one of the co-founders of the SDAP in 1869; a leader of the legal and illegal fighting by the Party during the period of Socialist law and brought about in some measure the founding of the Party's illegally published central document, *Der Sozialdemocrat*; from 1881-90 a member of the House of Delegates in Saxony; after 1889 a leading member of the II. International.

Bernstein, Eduard. Shop clerk. Publicist (*Neue Zeit*). Social Democrat, from 1890-1901; émigré in London, colleague of the theoreticians of revisionism; after 4 August 1914 no longer member of the Social Democratic Party of Germany.

Diefenbach, Hans (1884-1917). Medical doctor and Reserve officer, sympathetic to the cause of a German social democracy, wrote for *Neue Zeit*.

Ebert, Friedrich (1871-1925). Saddle maker, editor, Social Democrat. 1913-19 Party Chairman. From September 9, 1918-February 2, 1919 head of the provisional government, 1919-25 served as first President of Germany.

Jacob, Mathilde (1873-1943). Operated a secretarial service in Berlin for copying and translating. Secretary and confidential friend of Rosa Luxemburg, sympathetic to the cause of a German social democracy.

Jogiches, Leo (pseudonyms, among others: Otto Engelmann, Jan Tyszkaj) (1867-1919). Official in the Russian, Polish, German workers' movement. Emigrated to Switzerland. 1893 one of the founders of the Social Democratic Party of Poland (SDKP; after 1909 SDKPiL). Co-publisher of a Polish underground newspaper. After 1900 in Berlin. Co-founder in 1916 of the Spartacus Group. 1918 Member of the Central Committee of the KPD. March 1919 arrested and murdered in prison.

Kasprzak, Marcin (1860-1905). One of the founders of Party II. Proletariat. Emigrated to England. 1904 return to the Kingdom of Poland. Member of the

SDKPiL. Sentenced to death for carrying a firearm while defending an illegal printery. Executed on the 7th of September 1905.

Kautsky, Karl D (1854-1938). Writer. Social Democrat. Chief editor of *Die Neue Zeit* (1882-1917), well-known theoretician of the II. International, after 1910 a theoretician of centrism. In 1917 one of the founders of USPD; after the Russian October Revolution in 1917 became anti-Communist; during the German Revolution (1918-19) state secretary in the foreign office and chairman of the socialization commission.

Kautsky Luise D (1864-1944). Wife of Karl Kautsky. Writer. Longtime friend of Rosa Luxemburg.

Lenin (cover name for Vladimir Iljitsch Uljanow) (1870-1924). Russian revolutionary.

Levi, Paul (1883-1930). Attorney. Social Democrat. One of the defenders of Rosa Luxemburg in her trial court appearances. Active member of the Spartacus Group, 1918 member of the KPD.

Liebknecht, Karl (1871-1919). Attorney. Social Democrat. Strong supporter of Socialist Youth International. 1908-16 member of the Prussian Parliament, leading representative of the German Left. One of the founders of International Group (Spartacus Group) and in 1918 of the Spartacus Union. Responsible for preparation of *Rote Fahne* along with Rosa Luxemburg. A founder of the KPD. Murdered on 15 January 1919.

Liebknecht, Sophie Sonja (1884-1964). Art historian. Second wife of Karl Liebknecht.

Liebknecht, Wilhelm (1826-1900). Father of Karl Liebknecht. Founder of the SPD.

Lübeck, Gustav (1873). Typesetter. Entered into a marriage in name only with Rosa Luxemburg in 1898, divorced in 1903.

Luxemburg, Anna (1855-1932?). Sister of Rosa Luxemburg.

Luxemburg, Eliasz (Edward) (d. 1900). Father of Rosa Luxemburg.

Luxemburg, Jozef. Doctor of internal medicine and neurology in Warsaw. Brother of Rosa Luxemburg.

Luxemburg, Lina née Lowenstein (d. 1897). Mother of Rosa Luxemburg.

Luxemburg, Maksymillian (1860-1943). Businessman in Warsaw. Brother of Rosa Luxemburg.

Luxemburg, Mikolaj. Brother of Rosa Luxemburg, resided in London.

Mehring, Franz (1846-1919). Historian and publicist. Social Democrat. 1891-1913 worked for *Die Neue Zeit*. 1902-07 Chief editor of the *Leipziger Volkszeitung*. 1906-11 history teacher in the Central Party School in Berlin. From 1913-4 published *Sozialdemokratische Korrespondenz* together with Rosa Luxemburg and Julian Marchlewski, and in April 1915 published the first and only number of the journal *Die Internationale* together with Rosa Luxemburg. He belonged to the Gruppe Internationale (Spartacus Group). In 1917 member of the Prussian House of Delegates; co-founder of the Spartacus Union and the KPD.

Noske, Gustav (1868-1946). Basketmaker. Social Democrat with nationalistic tendencies. After 6 January 1919 troop commander in Berlin; connected to the Freikorps.

Pabst, Waldemar. Major, First Staff Officer of the Cavalry Guard-Protective Division. Organizer of the murder of Rosa Luxemburg and Karl Liebknecht.

Runge, Otto Wilhelm. Mercenary, carried out the murderous beatings of Rosa Luxemburg and Karl Liebknecht.

Scheidemann, Philipp (1865-1939). Typesetter. Social Democrat. From 1911 member of the leadership of the Social Democratic Party of Germany; active representative of opportunism, 1917-18 chairman of the SPD along with Friedrich Ebert; in October 1918 joined the government of Prince Max von Baden. Contributed significantly to the defeat of the November Revolution in 1918-19.

Souchon, Hermann W. Naval Lieutenant. Shot Rosa Luxemburg as she sat in an auto on 15 January 1919.

Witold (pseudonym for Feinstein, Wladyslaw) (1880-1938). Jurist, publicist, official of the Polish and international workers' movement.

Zetkin, Clara (1857-1933). Social Democrat. From 1892-1917 directed production of the Social Democratic journal, *Die Gleichheit*. Wrote for the journal *Die Internationale* and was one of the founders of the Group Internationale (Spartacus Union); from 1919 prominent member of the KPD.

Zetkin, Kostja (1885-1980). Medical doctor. Son of Clara Zetkin.

Chronology

1871   5 March, Rosa L. born in Zamóśc, the Russian part of Poland, fifth child of Eliasz and Lina Luksenburg. 1879 is sometimes listed as the birth year. (Her "Abitur" certificate of 1887 shows her age as seventeen.)

1873   The family Luksenburg moved to Warsaw, 16 Zlotastrasse.

1880   Attended the II. Mädchengymnasium in Warsaw, where she earned a "best student" "Abitur."

1887-88   Participated in a group studying illegal works of Polish literature. Participated in the group "Revolutionary Party of Proletarians."

1889   Emigrated to Switzerland, reported to police in Zurich-Oberstrass. The Second Internationale founded in Paris.

1890   Lived with Leo Jogiches (until 1906-7). The German SPD wins a 19.8% vote in the Reichstag elections but only 9% of the mandate.

1893-93   Publication debut with two Polish brochures for 1 May.

1893   Founded, with Leo Jogiches and others, the Social Democracy of the Kingdom of Poland (SDKP). At the International Socialist Workers' Congress in Zurich Rosa Luxemburg's mandate is not recognized.

1894   Until 1896 a reader for the monthly journal *Sprawa Robotnicza* ("Workers' Business").

1896   *Die Neue Zeit* published an article by Rosa Luxemburg for the first time. In it she entered into the international quarrel over the establishment of Poland as a national entity. Took part in the International Socialist Workers and Workplace Congress in London.

1897   Graduated magna cum laude with a doctorate in jurisprudence at the University of Zurich. Dissertation: "Die industrielle Entwicklung Polens." Mother died in Warsaw.

1898   Fake marriage to Gustav Lübeck in order to obtain Prusssian citizenship.

1898   Moved to Berlin. First Berlin residence at Cuxhavenerstrasse 2. Became member of SPD.

Until 1913-14 published in the *Leipziger Volkszeitung, Vorwärts, Die Neue Zeit* and other Social Democratic organs. Successful journeys to Upper Silesia to create dissent during Reichstag campaigns.

1899   Published "Sozialreform oder Revolution?" an argument against Eduard Bernstein's revisionism.

Delegate to the Social Democratic Party meeting in Hanover. Beginning of the Farmer's War.

1900   Took part in the Party meeting in Mainz. Spoke on the theme "Der Völkerfriede, der Militarismus, die Beseitigung der stehenden Heer" at the International Socialist Congress in Paris. Death of her father in Warsaw.

1901-03   Participation in international discussions within the Socialist movement over entry into middle-class governments, campaign strikes, terrorism, and Party crises, progress in Marxist theory. Took part in the Social Democratic Lübeck Party Day.

1902   Delegate to the Party Day in Munich. New residence in Berlin-Friedenau, Cranachstrasse 58 (until 1911).

1903   Tour as agitator in Saxony (Sachsengängerei) before the Reichstag elections.

Took part in the Party Day in Dresden.

Divorced Gustav Lübeck.

1904   Took part in the international Social Democratic Congress in Amsterdam.

Her article in *Die Neue Zeit*, "Organisationsfrage der russischen Sozialdeemokratie" was a polemic against Lenin's Party theory and the results of the II. Party Day of the Social Democratic Workers' Party of Russia (SDAPR).

Two months in prison in Zwickau for insult to the ruler.

Member of the International Socialist Office as the representative of the kingdom of Poland and Lithuania (SDKPiL) (until 1914).

1905   Outbreak of the first revolution in Russia. On 22 January: Bloody Sunday in St. Petersburg. Supported the Russian and Polish revolutionaries together with Leo Jogiches.

Took part in the Jena Party Day of the German Socialists.

Illegal trip to Warsaw. Took part in the revolution.

1906   Imprisoned on 4 March. In the Arretierungshaus am Rathaus until 28 June, then in Pawiak. Imprisoned in X Pavilion of the Warsaw citadel.

End of July a trip beyond St. Petersburg to Finnish Kuokkala.

Return to Germany in September. Her text "Massenstreik, Partei und Gewerkshaften," written in Kuokkala, published.

Took part in the Mannheim Party Day of the German Socialist Democracy.

Love affair with Kostja Zetkin (until 1909).

1907   Dissolution of relationship with Leo Jogiches.

Took part in London Party Day of the SDAPR. Commented on the consequences of the Russian Revolution.

Two months imprisonment in Berlin's Women's Prison on Barnimstrasse for inciting the public to use force.

Teacher of economic history and national economics in the Party's School of German Social Democracy in Berlin (until 1914).

Her text, *Einführung in die Nationalökonomie*, based on her school lectures, was published in book form in 1925 with the help of Paul Levi.

Took part in the I. International Conference of Socialist Women and in the International Socialist Congress in Stuttgart. Together with Lenin and Martow she supported Bebel's resolution against militarism and international conflicts.

1908   Delegate to the Social Democratic Party Day in Nuremberg.

Wrote a series of articles on "Die Nationalitätfrage und die Autonomie" for the journal, *Sozialdemokratische Rundschau*, published in Krakau under the leadership of Leo Jogiches.

Painting and sketching are a new passion.

1910   Several trips to gatherings in Upper Silesia, the Ruhr Valley, and in Baden to speak against the Prussian three-classes election. Pleaded for a political mass strike and anti-monarchism.

Disagreement and political break from Karl Kautsky and other representatives of the Party and the union, which took up a position against her demands for a mass strike and a democratic republic.

Took part in the international Socialist Congress in Copenhagen.

Co-initiator of several meetings of the Leftists within Germany's Social Democrats.

Took part in the Magdeburg Party Day.

Co-worker on the weekly paper, *Mlot* ("The Hammer," published by Leo Jogiches). Campaigned with representatives of the international Socialist Office against anti-Semitic agitation.

1911   Quarrel with Karl Kautsky and others about the illusion of peace. New trips to arouse the masses.

Delegate to the Jena Party Day of Social Democracy.

Polemical quarrel with Lenin and others about the SDAPR. Her demand: a single and democratic mass Party.

Moved to Berlin-Südende, Lindenstrasse 2.

In December a group tour through Saxony during the Reichstag election.

1912   In January at the Reichstag elections in Thuringia, Frankfurt/Main, and surrounding areas.

Took part in the Extraordinary International Socialist Congress in Basel.

Worked on the book, *Die Akkumulation des Kapitals*, which appears in 1913.

1913   Polemic against the comments of the Social Democratic Reichstag faction re the defensive pattern of the government.

Quarrel with Socialist reformists and centrists within Germany's Social Democracy.

Took part in Party Day in Jena.

Publisher, with Julian Marchlewski and Franz Mehring, of the *Social Democratic Correspondence*.

Installation of an herbarium that is enlarged in the following years.

1914   Three charges and two court appearances because of her talk against militarism and war and for a political mass strike. On 20 February she was sentenced to one year in prison by the Frankfurt state court. Sentence upheld 22 October by the highest court.

Liaison for a time with Paul Levi.

Took part in July in the "Russian Conference" of the International Socialist Office in Brussels in defense of peace.

World War I broke out on 1 August.

From September on gave advice about the first steps in the fight against the war and the unfettered freedom of the Party.

1915   In January a patient in the Auguste-Victoria Hospital in Berlin-Schöneberg as a result of abdominal pain.

After 18 February in the Berlin Women's Prison at Barnimstrasse 10 (until 18 February 1916).

Published the first number of the journal, *Die Internationale*, together with Clara Zetkin and Franz Mehring.

Worked on the text, *Krise der Sozialdemokratie*, which appeared in February 1916 in Zurich as a brochure under the pseudonym Junius.

Answer to critics of her argumentative work, *Die Akkumulation des Kapitals oder Was die Epigonen aus der Marxschen Theorie gemacht haben*, appears in 1921.

1916   Co-founder of the Spartacus Group.

Took part on 1 May in an anti-war demonstration in Potsdamerplatz.

Protested against the imprisonment and sentence of Karl Liebknecht for treason against the state.

On 8 July imposition of military protective custody.

After 10 July protective custody in the police prison on Alexanderplatz and in the Women's Prison on Barnimstrasse.

After 26 October protective custody in the Fortress Wronke.

1917   On 18 January expelled from the SPD.

In April the Spartacus Group and the USPD combined to protect their political-ideological and organizational independence.

Outbreak of the Russian "February Revolution" from 12-16 March.

On 18 June elected delegate to the International Socialist Conference, Stockholm, at which the imprisoned woman in protective custody could not take part.

On 22 July transfer from the Fortress Wronke into the prison in Breslau, Kletschkaustrasse.

Supported the revolutionary opposition in rebelling against the war and for a revolution in Germany.

Loss of her friend Hans Diefenbach, who died at the Front.

On the 7-8th of November the "October Revolution" in Russia.

Wrote numerous articles for the *Spartakusbriefe* (until 1918).

Made a translation of Wladimir Korolenko's autobiography, *Die Geschichte meines Zeitgenossen*, from Russian and wrote a literary historical introduction to the book. It appeared in 1919, published by Paul Cassirer.

1918   In September/October begins the manuscript, *Zur russischen Revolution*, with a polemic against Lenin, Trotzki, and the Bolsheviks. Never completed.

From 3 November an uprising of sailors in Kiel. The revolutionary movement spreads rapidly into the most important cities in Germany.

On 8 November freed from the Breslau prison.

From 10 November writes and edits *Rote Fahne* with Karl Liebknecht. In the following weeks she writes a number of basic articles on the course of the revolution and its tasks and goals.

On 11 November the capitulation of Germany.

On 14 December publication of the programmatic sketch, *Was will der Spartakusbund?*

30 December/1 January co-founding of the Communist Party of Germany.

Gave talks regarding its program and political situation. Rosa L. pleads to take part in the election to the national gathering.

Counter-revolutionary lust for murder and an anti-Bolshevistic psyched-up persecutory hunt for Rosa L. and Karl Liebknecht displayed on posters, flyers, and in the press, even in *Vorwärts*.

1919   On 5 January the German Worker's Party (DAP, later NSDAP) is founded. Soon afterwards its members include Alfred Rosenberg, Ernst Röhm, Rudolf Hess, and Adolf Hitler.

On 14 January her last article appears in *Rote Fahne*, "Die Ordnung herrscht in Berlin."

On 15 January Rosa Luxemburg and Karl Liebknecht are arrested at Mannheimerstrasse 43 by members of the Wilmersdorf Citizens Defense Corps and taken to the Eden Hotel on the Kurfürstendamm in Berlin. She is murdered by soldiers of the Free Corps of the Cavalry Guard Protective Division after a telephoned order by the Commander Captain Waldemar Pabst with Gustav Noske (after January Head Commander of Brandenburg and Commissioner in charge of defense questions in the Ebert-Scheidemann government).

Rosa Luxemburg is killed by blows from the weapon of the mercenary Otto Wilhelm Runge and shot by Naval Lieutenant Hermann W. Souchon and thrown into the Landwehrkanal from the Lichtenstein Bridge.

On 31 May discovery of the corpse of Rosa Luxemburg by canal worker Knebel between Freiarchen and S-Bahn Bridge. Chief of Police Ernst permits transport to the morgue in Hanoverstrasse. Gustav Noske imposes a ban on news reports.

On 1 June, upon Noske's order, the corpse is transported by military command to the garrison hospital at the troop training ground in Zossen.

On 2 June announcement in *Vorwärts* under the headline "The corpse of Rosa Luxemburg found?" Identified by Mathilde Jacob.

On 13 June she is buried in the cemetery in Berlin-Friedrichsfelde.

Fortress Wronke cell in which Rosa Luxemburg slept from 1916-17.

Lichtenstein Bridge over the Landwehrkanal, Berlin.

Leo Jogiches circa 1900.

Rosa Luxemburg, 1910.

Rosa Luxemburg circa 1912.

978-0-595-48962-6
0-595-48962-1